cook simply,
live fully

Also by Yasmin Fahr

Keeping It Simple

Boards & Spreads

cook simply, live fully

flexible, flavorful recipes for any mood

yasmin fahr

HARPER

An Imprint of HarperCollins*Publishers*

To everyone reading and cooking from this book.

Thank you for trusting me with your time and dinner, whether it's eaten on your lap, sitting on the floor, or around a table.

I hope you enjoy!

contents

a little hello!

People do crazy things for love. Upend their lives, quit jobs, move to other countries, all to chase the joy, adventure, and sense of completion another person incites.

Welcome to a brief story about me. It was September 2021, and I was on a solo eight-day trip to a small island in the Balearics off the coast of mainland Spain. I had been eyeing a hotel there for the past couple of years, but with some life things and the pandemic, my trips kept getting postponed. Like many during this time, I was suffering from exhaustion, burnout from an intense work project, and feeling pretty down and defeated about life. It wasn't great—but this story isn't going in a depressing direction, I promise! After crying in broad daylight while walking along the Hudson River and talking to my sister (I mean serious ugly crying, with no sunglasses to hide anything), I decided I needed to get away for some perspective and, four days before my flight took off, magically pulled together this trip without spending an insane amount of money. Off to Spain I went.

And it was the single best decision I've made in my life.

I spent days reading book after book, swimming in the clear, warm water, eating heaping plates of jamón and pan con tomate, and drinking lots of wine and vermut, much of which was grown and produced on that gorgeous island. It was idyllic, to say the least, and exactly what I needed. One windy afternoon, as most tended to be there, I sat at a tiny, hidden cala whose beach was populated by only one other person, a lovely older woman with long gray hair. As I attempted to walk over the mounds of dried algae that barred entry to the water (perhaps one reason it was so deserted), she kindly warned me about the jellyfish (and maybe that's another). We began chatting, and she told me she had retired here from England and loved it. *Good for her*, I thought.

The next day I saw her again, looking so relaxed and happy, and we waved to each other and chatted a bit. As the sun was dipping down, I watched as she wrapped herself in a turquoise sarong and climbed up the side of the cliff by the water's edge, precariously walking along a skinny, rocky path until she reached the mouth of the cala, where the blue-green water melted into the seemingly never-ending expanse of the sea. She leaned against a giant rock, bracing her back against it as the wind whipped her hair back, the sarong flying behind her like a cape, almost looking like an old-fashioned wooden mermaid carved on the prow of a ship, facing the wild, turbulent water. She looked so strong and free, with a raw, unbridled connection with nature, that I felt a sense of awe watching her. It filled me with a rush to do the same, which I did later, walking barefoot along the pebbly path. My walk was wobblier and more apprehensive than hers, as I was sure I was going to get blown over, but when I finally made it, standing on the edge of the cliff, the wind barreling against me, I had one of those moments where everything suddenly felt clear.

During this time, I also learned a lot about myself, realizing that I need time alone to recharge just as much as I love being around people.
I paid more attention to my moods and needs and realized that was also how I decide what to cook: It all depends on the energy I have and how I want to feel at the end of the meal.

I was so sure of the change I needed to make that when I returned to my beach blanket, I immediately grabbed my phone and texted my friend Ian, who was thinking of moving to NYC: "Do you want to sublet my apartment? I want to be the naked lady on the beach!!" (Did I forget to mention she was naked?)

In some strange, inexplicable way, I fell in love with the feeling that this island gave me. I realized I needed to simplify and quiet down my life, which had felt very "busy" of late, with things that didn't bring me joy. I was moving through routines, eating and drinking too much and going through the motions, but feeling empty and unfulfilled. I wanted to spend more time outside in nature and enjoy my life more. We all have a happy place, whether it's a city, an island, or an activity that makes us feel alive and offers a brief respite from the daily complications and requirements of being an adult. That moment made me realize I had been missing this, and I knew I needed to chase that feeling.

The next few months were filled with the obvious anxiety you might imagine, but when

my landlords kindly let me out of my lease early without penalty, I took it as a sign. Somewhat impulsively, I decided to move to Miami, reasoning that being by the water would be a good transitional step until I could figure out a way to get back to Spain. It seemed like a solid plan, until, for reasons beyond my control and understanding, it was impossible for me to find a place there. Every lease I was about to sign fell through, with owners disappearing after I put in an application or receiving a last-minute offer to purchase the condo I wanted to rent—it just wasn't working out. Whether you believe in fate or not, it felt a bit fated that I had to wait, even though I had already given up my apartment in New York. So, with all my stuff in storage except my knife kit and a small suitcase of warm-weather clothing, I found myself back in Menorca.

I spent almost seven weeks on an unplanned solo cooking and writing retreat, diving into this book with a clear, happy mind. As I bounced around different kitchens, learning how to operate new ovens and stovetops and navigating butcher shops and fishmongers in poor Spanish, the tone of this book—simple, flexible, accessible cooking—took shape.

I believe that cooking according to your mood and energy level—prioritizing what you need—is a form of self-care. Rather than doing what I "should" do or what would be "smart," I do what I need to in that moment, even if it means throwing out a previous plan. And when that happens, I don't let myself feel guilty about it—instead, I'm proud of myself for doing what was best for me.

For example, I might pick up some beautiful potatoes at the farmers' market in the morning and get all excited about this idea I had of boiling them, then smashing them to make a crispy and crunchy potato salad of sorts with local capers I just bought. Then the day goes by and dinnertime rolls around, and the idea of all of these steps and cleaning up feels like it's just not going to happen. And it doesn't. Instead, I make something super simple and save the potatoes for the next day. Hello, new me! I am now a flexible and adaptable person, forgiving myself for being human rather than holding myself to arbitrary and self-inflicted rules and goals. (Just kidding, I'm still a work in progress.)

And that's ultimately the goal of this book: to provide you with recipes for whatever need you have, whenever you have it, no matter how you're feeling. I want to help make you a confident and intuitive home cook so that you can breezily create a meal out of pantry staples, composing simple yet deeply flavorful dishes that you're excited about eating—and having lots of fun along the way, because that's what food is all about. You're going to find a lot of advice, too, small tidbits and suggestions for swaps to help make your life easier in the kitchen, which you are welcome to skim over and ignore until you're ready to download all that information. And, of course, you'll find 112 concrete, foolproof recipes that you can follow to the letter if you're not in the mood to think or learn—I totally get that, too.

You'll also probably find that I use the word "simple" a lot, like a lot, a lot (along with "lemony" and "bright"), because that's how I want this book to feel: like a seamless, sunny, and simple addition to your life. That's what my Menorca time inspired me to do: slow down and try to remove the clutter and the noise and the excess so that the simple goodness of food can shine.

I find that in this way, when we cook simply, we feel full, both in life and in our bellies, because we are giving ourselves what we need.

Hope you enjoy!
~yasmin xx

how to use this book to make your life easier

A friend once told me that when she gets a new cookbook, she reads it start to finish, immediately marking what she wants to make, and then cooks her way through it before moving on to the next cookbook, a habit that I love.

As someone who collects cookbooks, I love reading through them, holding them in my hands, getting to know the author and learning from them. I also have some that serve more as beauty books, ones that I was gifted or meant to read but somehow just never did—these are stacked on top of my bookshelf, looking great, with nary a creased binding in sight. So while I'm honored to be part of your cookbook collection, I *really* hope this book isn't a top-of-the-bookshelf one for you. That would probably make me sadder than a bad review. *Cook Simply, Live Fully* isn't meant to sit pristinely on your bookshelf, looking pretty, even though she is quite beautiful.

I want this book to be your kitchen companion and buddy, kind of like if you were going to text me with the question, *What should I make for dinner?* I want it to be what you turn to when you're feeling tired and blue *and* when you've had a glorious night's rest and are ready to take on the world—the best feeling, isn't it? As you flip through the book, reading it front to back or stopping at whatever catches your eye, please write notes in the margins, cross out what you don't love, replacing it with what you do (I won't be offended, I promise!). Dog-ear the pages, use stickies, or whatever your style is to make this book feel yours. It's one that's meant to be used, to be loved, and to show signs of wear, full of wrinkles and spills, because these are also all signs of Real Life. And that's what these recipes are meant to help you navigate, from the times when washing a cutting board or pan feels near impossible to the moments when you wake up wanting to cook a feast for your nearest and dearest.

This is why when people ask me what I usually make for dinner, I pause, my mind draws a total blank, and I say, "I have no idea, it all really depends on how I feel." (I don't think anyone has found this response helpful or insightful to date.) Though hopefully that will change, as that's how these recipes are organized. You pick the section you want to explore based on how you feel, or, to be more exact, the energy level and motivation you have and how you want to feel after you eat.

Here's what I mean by all of that.

energy level + motivation
how much energy do i have to make dinner?

1 lap dinners

The section contains recipes for when you're dead tired, as they require little to no prep and come together in more or less 15 to 20 minutes. Think all types of noodles, one-pot soups, and quickly cooked vegetables that rely on condiments for fast flavor, plus the easiest sheet pan meals of chicken or salmon with low-prep vegetables. You'll probably be using kitchen shears to "prep" anything. You'll also likely be surprised at how deeply flavorful these meals end up being, considering how absurdly easy they are to make.

2 coffee table dinners

Here you'll find classic weeknight recipes for evenings when you've still got some energy, but you don't want to spend more than 30 to 45 minutes in the kitchen or for it to be a Big Thing. There will be lots of sheet pan dishes like roast chicken thighs and vegetables, and fairly simple (yet flavorful) soups, stews, and pastas. At the very end, there's also a cheat sheet for roasting and cooking vegetables so you can add another sheet pan to the oven or quickly cook some greens in a skillet to bulk up a meal. You won't need more than one or two pots/sheet pans, and prep time remains minimal. We want you in and out of that kitchen with a great meal in hand.

3 at the dinner table

This last chunk of recipes is waiting for you when have a spurt of energy and feel excited to take on a little more work or are looking to feed a crowd. Some require a bit more effort and time, like Easy Baked Lasagna with Broccolini (page 194), just because of the nature of lasagna, but they are as streamlined as possible. Don't worry, I won't have you in the kitchen for hours, leaving you burned out a quarter of the way through when that flame of excitement dies, looking around in misery at the massive mess around you—I've done this to myself, many, many times, and it's no fun. These dishes might require some marinating time or a little more prep work, but nothing will take more than an hour or so. Plus, you'll find some big bowl salads and lots of vegetable snacks and side dishes that can be eaten on their own or added on to any meal in this book for a larger spread.

mood wise

how do i want to feel after i eat?

While energy dictates my cooking, so does my mood—do I want something comforting and cozy? Something light that will be filling but not too heavy? These cravings usually tend to align with the weather, but sometimes I want something light and comforting on a hot day, like a cool (not sweaty) hug. These recipes are loosely arranged within each section from lighter and brighter dishes to warmer and cozier ones, and loosely follow the four seasons. Of course, these are all open to your personal interpretation.

some things to know as you flip through . . .

I like to think of my recipes as a road map. If you follow them exactly, you'll get to your destination, no problem. But if you've been down this road before and know a shortcut, or have a different route you prefer, then do whatever works best for you; you just might get a slightly different end result. No matter what, I would read each recipe through to familiarize yourself with the steps before you start cooking. Plus, keep in mind that . . .

→ **Every oven recipe is set to 400°F** so you can easily swap vegetables and proteins within a recipe or add another sheet pan without having to do math (thank goodness!).

→ **The vegetable skillet + roasting chart** (see page 113) is a quick reference guide on how to prep vegetables and cook them in the most basic of ways, so you can easily swap and play as noted above. (Maybe dog-ear that page or add a sticky tab.)

→ **Wine pairing chart!!** (see page 117.) I'm so excited about this, and hope you like it, too. Sommelier Allegra Angelo set up recommendations based on the dominant ingredients in this book (check the recipe titles if you're wondering what they are), so you can take those notes to your local wine shop or search online.

→ **I keep an old-school magenta ruler in my kitchen** when I'm developing recipes and use it to randomly check pieces of this or that to make sure they match up to what I'm writing. I thought this built-in tool would save you the trouble of keeping a ruler around or eyeballing it, although that's fine, too! (See the spine of the book and page 111 for the ruler.)

→ **The most important thing** is to pay attention to what's happening in your skillet or sheet pan by looking at your food and noting cues like color, texture, and aroma in addition to the cooking time, because every oven, stovetop, and kitchen is different.

have fun with these recipes, please!

essential tools and ingredients

You really don't need a lot, and I'm not just saying that, I promise. There are no blenders, mixers, or other electric tools used, as I have a low-tech approach to cooking. With some wooden spoons, a couple of pots/sheet pans, and a cutting board, we can make pretty much any recipe here.

Cutting boards (preferably wood, which is nice on your knives): 1 large + a separate small one for "smelly" food, like garlic/onions so they don't make your other foods smell like garlic

A good (and sharp!) **chef's knife**

A **paring knife** for cutting small things

12-inch cast-iron skillet (they are inexpensive, last a lifetime if taken care of, and can be used for so many things) or other heavy skillet

Dutch oven or large pot with a tight-fitting lid (Le Creuset is an investment, but I've had mine for 12+ years, and it's still a beauty)

1 or 2 sturdy half sheet pans (18 by 13-inch) (I love Nordic Ware)

Microplane, zester, or cheese grater (makes grating garlic, ginger, citrus zest, and cheese so easy)

Wooden spoons or rubber spatulas (I call for these as they are gentler on your pots/pans and won't scratch them)

some helpful things if you're willing to expand your collection

Kitchen shears Different from scissors, I have one pair exclusively used for food and keep them very sharp. These are great for snipping herbs, meat, or anything you don't feel like cutting (hello, lap dinners!).

Fish spatula Even though it's called a "fish spatula," this flexible metal spatula can be used for flipping meat, burgers, pancakes, and so on.

Fun mixing bowls, and fun bowls in general I like collecting brightly colored ones even though I often use my plain metal or glass ones, too.

Pepper mill It's very helpful for grinding fresh pepper. I've had a Peugeot one for over ten years and still use it; an investment, but worth it.

A 9 by 13-inch glass baking dish or braising dish You can use a sheet pan or Dutch oven in a pinch, but these are useful.

Meat thermometer You don't need one for this book, but it keeps any raw-meat worries at bay.

ingredients + spices + some notes

My pet peeve, and perhaps yours, too, is buying a small (or large) jar of something—be it a spice, condiment, or dried good—only to use a tiny portion of it in a recipe and then find it hibernating in the back of my fridge/cabinet/drawer months or even years later. My promise to you is this: Anything you buy for a recipe in this book, you'll use in at least three other recipes (if it's something small, at least two recipes). That way, you don't have to search online for recipes that use a specific ingredient, or promise yourself you will but never get around to it (welcome to my life).

not tooo many dried herbs + spices (just 6!)

You'll be surprised how much you can do with just the ones listed here. I keep them in small salt cellars, much like a masala dabba, so I can easily reach for them when cooking.

Ground cumin/
  cumin seeds
Red pepper flakes

Dried oregano
Ground turmeric
Ground sumac

Piménton (smoked
  paprika) (see note on
  page xxi)

some other pantry/fridge staples

Dijon mustard
Dried pasta (various
  shapes)
White miso paste

Feta (preferably Bulgarian)
  and/or Parmesan (see
  note on page xxi)
Panko bread crumbs

Harissa
Canned tomatoes
  and tomato paste
Soy sauce

on vinegars
(sherry, red wine, apple cider, balsamic)

The world of vinegars is vast, and you don't need to buy all of these—experiment with the ones you like. Sherry vinegar is my go-to—it adds great flavor in dressings or as a finishing touch to dishes, and a splash in tomato sauce can work wonders. Apple cider is a bit fruitier and less acidic than sherry, so I find that's a nice way to switch it up, but you might need a touch more apple cider vinegar for more acidity, so adjust as needed. Same with the other vinegars, you might need a little more or less if you swap them. Taste and see.

  Swap citrus juice, like lemon or lime, for vinegar, depending on what you have on hand. (Lemon and lime have a similar acidity, so you can swap those more easily.) Vinegar, along with citrus juice, gives a bright, acidic finish to dishes, which is often what they need, rather than salt, when they taste imbalanced.

on...

canned beans and chickpeas
These are all no-salt-added and should be drained and rinsed before use (I know some people love using the canning liquid to thicken soups or pastas, but I'm a rinser).

garlic When I say 3 garlic cloves, I'm referring to 3 large ones, the chunky ones, usually on the outside of the head of garlic. If you find yourself with smaller middle cloves, then use 2 of those in place of 1 larger clove. Also, on that point, the strength of garlic varies depending on how it's cut—the more you chop it (think minced or grated), the stronger the flavor will be; when it's thinly sliced or smashed, it will give a subtle garlic flavor to the dish and won't be as strong.

ginger I don't peel my ginger, but you can if you'd like. I always grate it, as it can be stringy if not chopped very, very finely, and even then can be overly strong in bites. Store ginger, cut into 1- to 3-inch pieces, in the freezer to grate from frozen as needed.

jasmine/basmati rice Rinse your rice in a sieve under cold running water, using your hand to agitate the grains, until the water dripping out the bottom is clear rather than cloudy. You can also soak your rice, if you have the foresight, for an hour or two before cooking.

olive oil The only oil you'll find in this book is olive oil; I use an extra-virgin olive oil for cooking and a nicer, more expensive extra-virgin for finishing. (There are times when you might think, *a sesame oil would be nice here,* but if you're already noticing that, you'll probably sub it in anyway, and please do.) I love collecting different finishing oils, which can be drizzled on a finished dish, or sliced tomatoes, or cheese at the last minute and give tons of flavor, or served for dipping bread in.

parmesan/parmigiano-reggiano While freshly grating mounds of fluffy Parmigiano Reggiano is best, I'll admit that I often buy the coarsely grated Parmigiano-Reggiano option at the cheesemonger section of supermarkets as they do the work for me, which is great on tired nights, and what I mean when I refer to Parmesan (I'm not talking about the commercial brands of Parmesan, whether in a can or plastic bag—avoid those at all costs, as they have additives that will make your pasta clumpy). I tend to have both a whole wedge and some grated Parmesan in my little cheese drawer so that I can pull whatever I need, depending on my energy level.

paprika The paprika used in the book is what I found in Spain, which is called piménton, essentially smoked paprika that's common there. It comes in three forms, and I tend to buy the picante, which is a bit spicy, but you can use whatever you like or find.

salt For cooking, you need a good-quality everyday salt and a flaky finishing salt, if you'd like (see page 40 for more on salt choices). When the recipe calls for "salt," it's your cooking salt to turn to.

washing vegetables To be fully transparent, I often don't wash vegetables unless there is visible dirt on them or they are from a farmers' market. But if you're washing yours, they should all be washed and dried (unless they're cooking in water) and ready to go before you start cooking.

turtle life

my tips for good eating and living

When I first met Rolando Cortés at an after-party in Brooklyn for a mezcal documentary my friend Kaj helped produce, someone asked him what his favorite mezcal was, and he said something like, "I have one that I drink when I'm happy, one when I'm sad, and one to celebrate. You have to find the mezcal that fits your mood." (Hello, synchronicity and this book! Which, at the time, was with my agent—hi, Kari!—in proposal form.)

Waking up in the center of Oaxaca after a fun night out a few months later during my traveling cook days, on a hot, clear morning with a thin layer of pollution breezing through the city, I was not in peak form. My friend Nicole popped out of the stairwell and onto the roof where I was waiting for her and burst out laughing because I was lying on the couch, my feet hanging over one end, trying to compose myself and mentally prepare for a twelve-hour day of tasting mezcal.

We were meeting Moni Cortés and Matt Morrison from Casa Cortés, run by the Cortés family, who have been making mezcal in Oaxaca since the 1840s. We visited mezcaleros outside the city, driving through long stretches of land and down bumpy roads to learn about artisanal and ancestral methods of distilling the spirit, which opened my eyes to the complexity of this seemingly simple product. There is a deep emotional connection between mezcal and Oaxacan tradition and family; it's a part of both everyday life and the most sacred moments. (I'm getting to its connection with the book—bear with me, please.)

Much like wine, the terroir, growing methods, makers, and type of plant influence the taste of the final product. And also like wine, some industrial and commercial mezcals are made cheaply and quickly, pumping out bottles and using methods that damage natural resources, focusing more on the immediate rush to deliver than the future. The places we visited work in harmony with nature, moving slowly and simply to create something special that's worth savoring. As Rolando said, "Mezcal teaches us to respect Mother Earth and to be thankful for all she has to give us."

My experiences during this traveling period kept bringing me back to this theme of slowing down and connecting with nature (it felt a bit more like, *Hurry up and get the point already, Yaz!* than subtle hints). Sometimes in Menorca, I would sit and watch the turtles roam around, whether on the beach or tree-lined paths. And, goodness, I don't know how they get anywhere or manage to do anything. They have a level of chill that I can only dream of achieving. As much as I try, I find it really hard to slow down and live that turtle-like life when doing so feels so counter to the speed of our world, especially as a former New Yorker, where my speed and efficiency were sources of pride.

As embarrassing as it is to admit, I sometimes forget that nature also moves at that turtle-like pace, including the many people and networks that work really hard to get food to me, as I'm so used to having every ingredient available to me whenever I want it. It felt wild to me that during the photo shoot for this book, Broccolini was sold out in five different LA grocery stores—how could that be?! Same with dill—it couldn't be harvested because of the out-of-character rain LA was experiencing at the time. This incited a moment of panic because I had assumed I'd be able to get these ingredients, not considering that they needed to be grown in nature—it didn't matter what I wanted or expected, it wasn't happening. And maybe it was a good thing I couldn't get exactly what I wanted, when I wanted it, as I had to be more flexible (I added way more swaps in the book after that). Though it didn't stop me from wanting to stomp my feet, stare up at the sky, and groan, *Why me?!!* (I'm not a perfect person by any means, and I'm okay with that.)

Back in Oaxaca, deep in thought while sipping on mezcal, I wondered out loud, how do you explain to the world that the production of something like this takes time? It can't be pumped out and turned into an efficient machine, ready whenever we want it. Similarly, how can we expect to grow food and raise animals to match that pace? It probably wouldn't be done well or carefully, just like when we rush through our lives— that's never when I do my best work or feel like I'm fully there for the people I care about. Maybe it's good for us to wait a bit for the things we want and appreciate them when they *are* available, knowing the time and care it took to make them. This pains me to say, as patience has never been my strong suit.

While I attempt to navigate a more turtle-like life, moving slowly while still existing in a fast-moving world, I don't have answers for these larger questions—please let me know if you do! But I can offer the following thoughts, which have no basis in anything other than my own meandering life experience.

→ slow down and expect less

Set the bar low. Just kidding, but also not really. I learned to love that in Menorca, the butcher shop would close at 1 or 2 p.m., and very little was open on Sunday. Was it annoying when I wanted to test a meatball recipe again the same day but couldn't buy more meat? Yes. And did I feel like I was "wasting time" not being able to try it again? Yes. But then I ended up going for a long walk by the sea and trying the recipe again the next day, and I actually think that little bit of space was good for me to reflect on what I wanted to change. There was no *real* rush (is there ever?), so why was I putting that pressure on myself and getting worked up for no reason?

→ eat food that has been messed with as little as possible

This extends to heavily processed food or food that can't be quickly traced back to its original form (the Michael Pollan quote, "Don't eat anything your great-grandmother wouldn't recognize as food," comes to mind). Shop at places that put thought and care into what they make—choosing a local bakery making fresh bread, versus buying packaged sliced bread from the grocery store that's full of preservatives. Maybe it's because I work alone so much of the time, but my favorite moments in the day are the ones I spend chatting with people at bakeries, butchers, and grocery stores. I go overboard in Menorca, trying to keep my meals as much from the island as possible, and you don't have to go to that extreme, but it is nice to support the people who live near you.

→ same goes for buying meat + fish

Look for good-quality meat, and by that I mean meat from animals that were fed well and cared for, and that got to spend time outside—all things we hope for ourselves,

too (see page 178 for more on chicken). Shopping at a farmers' market, or somewhere that thoughtfully sources meat or fish, is usually the most reliable (albeit pricier) way to source quality protein that leaves minimal damage in its wake. I find that my body needs a certain amount of meat to feel good, so I source it well and round out my meals with lots of vegetables, grains, and legumes, which is kind of how this book is set up.

⇢ fruits + vegetables, too

When I finally moved to Miami, there wasn't a farmers' market that Barb and I could safely drive to—Barb was my flame-red, street-legal golf cart—so I shopped only at grocery stores. I deeply missed getting excited about the first appearance of seasonal vegetables, when I would get that buzzy, little-kid feeling of something I've been waiting for finally arriving. I became complacent about grocery shopping, even though Barb brought me an immense amount of joy, feeling like it was another thing to check off my list, which wasn't great as it's one of my favorite things to do, especially whenever I feel blue. For the most part, a lot of the grocery-store vegetables were lacking in flavor compared to the farmers' market produce that I was used to, making me realize how lucky I was to have had access to it, as it's not readily available for everyone. Though I did have a fun interaction with a very kind man working in the produce aisle as he complained about a demanding customer wanting the exact apple she had the previous day, "The apple you ate yesterday probably won't look exactly like the one you eat today," and that's a good thing. Apparently I'm not the only one who forgot how food is grown!

⇢ please don't worry too much about any of this

I was a vegetarian twice in my life, for a total of about two years—*once* after a nutrition course in college, and then after a food policy class in graduate school, where I was thoroughly frightened about factory farming and elements of our food system. Truth be told, I became annoying to be around—I was always worried about the sourcing of the meat and dairy, and was picky when eating out. I tried not to lecture those I ate with, but my face is very expressive—it took away the fun of food for me (and likely for those around me), so I stopped worrying so much. I now make the best choices for me in that moment, trying to be as responsible and thoughtful as I can be. So, take these thoughts as you will because I don't want to cause you any more stress or anguish in this world, especially when it comes to the joy that is food and eating. I don't want you to feel pressured or guilty about any of your shopping choices or if you don't live near a farmers' market. Make the best, most affordable choice for you and move on because . . .

➙ the most important thing is— the happiness factor!

During one of the two times I lived in LA, I was shopping at the grocery store, standing in front of the bulk food section, during that time of year when the first holiday music comes on and it still feels exciting because it's been almost a year since it last filled the airwaves. All of a sudden, I heard "Yaz?" It was my sister, staring at me from the end of the aisle (she lives in LA). She was randomly at the grocery store near me, and when she saw someone dancing in the aisle, she thought, *Who's that weirdo? Oh right, it's my sister.*

I do this super-embarrassing dance when I get excited—it's more like a little hop and bounce than a full-on dance. It's that little bit of joy that hits without me realizing I'm doing it. (Yes, in many ways I'm like a small child, unable to control my body.)

Whether you eat meat or not, enjoy dairy or not, drink wine or not, if you're happy and enjoying yourself, then I think that counts way more than worrying about "doing the right thing" or what's "good for you." The stuff that makes your heart sing is what you need to chase in life, and food has the ability to do just that, if you let it.

lap
dinners

1

i am very tired,
please make this easy + quick

*recipes for when you're dead tired,
don't want to chop a thing, and are
about to open that delivery app*

As someone who loves food, dreams about it, and gets overly excited about it, there are still nights and days when the last thing I want to do is make dinner. That's when it's more like, *What can I easily and quickly make without having to think or clean a cutting board, because that's simply not happening.*

And I think that's totally understandable, even if you love food—and even more so if you're new to the cooking game. Sometimes figuring out a meal can feel like a chore. Life isn't always photo-worthy meals and candlelit dinner tables full of invigorating conversation or endless laughter with friends; sometimes it's more like, *Oh sh*t, what's for dinner?*

The recipes in this section are more along the lines of "Let me pour myself a generous glass of wine while I binge-watch my comfort shows and see what I can throw together." We all have our go-to, bottom-of-the-barrel dinners, and here's a collection of mine. These are easy and quick, and don't involve a cutting board or traditional measuring tools (see more on the next few pages). They're mostly meant to serve two to four people, though you can easily scale down for one person. For this reason, you can make them anywhere—be it your own kitchen, a poorly stocked rental house, the apartment of a friend who never cooks, or wherever else you might find yourself in a state of hunger and exhaustion. This can also happen after a long day in the sun!

measurements

In this section, unlike the other two, you'll find that precise measurements are
not given in the traditional way. Everything is much more casual and off the cuff,
so you can spoon things out of jars, drizzle oil, and season directly in the pan. I
understand that not using traditional measuring cups or spoons might sound
odd, or feel uncomfortable at first, but during my time as a traveling cook, I had a
revelation: I was in the UK, testing recipes at my cousin Leyla's house in Brighton.
She walked into the kitchen, and when she saw me use a measuring cup, said,
"Oh, that's funny, when they call for a cup, I just use one of these," and grabbed a
teacup from the shelf. Mind you, she's a phenomenal cook, and it made me think–
she made a lot of sense. I understand that measuring tools were likely created for
consistency in recipes so everyone's cup was the same, but wouldn't it be much
easier if we could just grab the nearest cup or spoon and use that? Especially if
the measuring spoons are dirty, because they are seriously such a pain to clean
by hand.

   And while I put a lot of thought and effort into my recipes, they aren't high-
maintenance, so a little bit more or less here or there won't make a huge difference.
(I do strictly measure everything when testing, and have others test the recipes,
too.) These recipes are intentionally forgiving and flexible because I would much
rather you enjoy the cooking process than worry about it being perfect.

This is roughly the spoon size I'm using for all of these. It's on the smaller end, not
a giant soup spoon or a small demitasse/teaspoon, but somewhere in the middle.
Rummage through the drawers, place it on top of this, and find one that comes as
close as you can, but no worries if it's a bit off.

olive oil amounts

When I tell you to add olive oil to a pan in "waves," I mean like the waves you learned about in science class. Move the bottle in a wavelike motion with a gentle flick of the wrist. One wave is moving across the pan/pot from left to right (or right to left if that's your preference); two would be reversing and going back right to left. Sometimes you need two travels across, sometimes three. But if you're adding olive oil to a pot, then I'll say to do a spiral, kind of like a snail shell, moving from the outer edge of the bowl in smaller and smaller rings toward the center. Some olive oil glugs out faster than others, so if that's your bottle, know that in a pan, there should be enough oil that the bottom is slick with a thin layer (tilt the pan to spread it out), and, if you're coating ingredients with oil, they should glisten lightly all over.

salting + seasoning

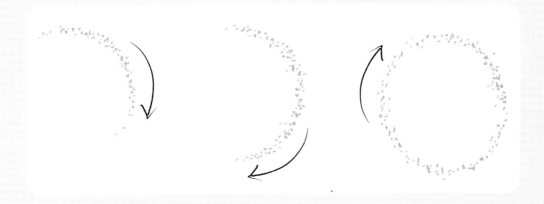

You'll see me call for "circles" or "waves" of salt. This means you pinch salt between your thumb, forefinger, and middle finger and circle the pot, releasing it, like a full moon or even a half-moon (like above), or moving in a wavelike motion across the pan (much like the olive oil). This should not be fistfuls of salt; you're merely releasing enough to lightly sprinkle it over everything, rather than dumping it in. Think of it more like a cute snow shower that lightly coats the ground than a blizzard. And if you get to the end of the circle or wave and still have some of the salt you pinched up, you don't have to release it. Start paying attention to the circles and see, by the finished dish, if you'd rather use more or less next time, then adjust accordingly (see page 40 for more on seasoning). For spices, you can shake them directly into the dish or spoon them out before adding them—those are the directions I will give—depending on your preference and setup.

P.S. The key for recipes where ratios are important—say, when you're cooking rice—is consistency. If you use a teacup to measure the rice, then use that same cup to measure the water for it—it's only the ratio that needs to be consistent. If you utterly hate this plan, then use 1 tablespoon for a spoonful (¼ spoonful is roughly ¼ to ½ teaspoon) and 1 cup for a teacup, and know that 2 waves is about 2 tablespoons.

skillet eggs with asparagus + feta (or parmesan)

This is a quick skillet meal that has the sopping-up-runny-yolks-with-bread action, so it's filling and interactive in the best way. If asparagus isn't in season, then cut up Broccolini or another quick-cooking vegetable (see page 110 for ideas) with kitchen shears and use that instead. If you're a garlic lover, adding some grated garlic along with the spices would also be nice, as would topping it with some harissa or your favorite hot sauce.

Serves 2

Olive oil

1 bunch asparagus, ends snapped off, stalks snipped into bite-size pieces

Salt

Ground cumin

Red pepper flakes

4 eggs

½ cup crumbled feta or grated Parmesan

Handful of fresh cilantro, parsley, basil, mint, or dill, gently torn

1 lemon, halved

Freshly cracked black pepper

Bread or delicate greens, for serving

Heat the broiler with a rack 6 inches from the heat source. Drizzle 2 waves of olive oil (or enough to coat with a thin layer) into a 12-inch ovenproof skillet over medium-high heat until shimmering. Add the asparagus, season with a half-moon of salt, and stir, then cook, undisturbed, until it becomes a vibrant green, about 2 minutes. Add a half-moon of cumin and red pepper flakes, stir to combine, and cook for 1 minute more.

Turn off the heat, then use a wooden spoon to make four wells in the asparagus, spaced a little apart, and crack an egg into each. Top with half the cheese and place under the broiler until the egg whites are firm and don't jiggle when you shake the pan, about 4 minutes.

Top with the remaining cheese and torn herbs, and squeeze half the lemon over everything. Finish with black pepper and serve with bread or delicate greens and the remaining lemon half to use as needed.

bread + cheese (aka noon-e-paneer)

I will not take up too much of your time expressing my deep love for Bulgarian feta, but I *am* going to say that when I moved to Miami and was struggling to find a good source, I checked a bag (something I usually avoid at all costs) after visiting my dad in Boston so I could bring back a large box of it. It was well wrapped in plastic with some duct tape to secure it, but not so much that it would look suspicious. My love runs deep.

I grew up eating this meal with my dad as a late breakfast pretty much every Saturday and Sunday, with a fresh sourdough baguette, herbs, cheese, and tomatoes all set out. It's a simple meal, one with little prep, yet it's unbelievably satisfying and can be eaten any time of year. And it's not too different from pan con tomate (see page 22), which is also an excellent no-brainer meal. Or simply slice toast, drizzle with olive oil, and top with an amazing sliced tomato and great salt—if I could eat in-season tomatoes, good bread, and cheese for the rest of my life, I would indeed be a happy lady. You can make any adjustments you like here; for example, swap out the tomatoes for some walnuts and honey, if that's your thing.

Serves 1 or 2

A generous hunk of soft, creamy cheese (I always vote for Bulgarian feta)

Great sourdough bread, toasted, or a fresh baguette, torn or sliced

1 to 2 heirloom tomatoes, or 1 pint Campari, cherry, or Sungold tomatoes (you do have to slice these, I'm sorry, please don't be mad!)

A handful of soft fresh herbs, such as basil, parsley, cilantro, or mint

Set out all the ingredients on a large cutting board, a plate, or a variety of plates and make little sandwiches. If you'd like more direction, spread the cheese on the bread, then top with tomatoes and herbs to make little open-faced sandwiches.

springy arugula pesto pasta with crispy chickpeas

When I was a luxury hotel reviewer, part of my job was to test the bar experience (truly difficult work here), which included the bar snacks. The snacks at a tropical beach bar in Central America have always stuck with me. They served housemade crispy chickpeas, ones that were crunchy and full of spice, with just the right amount of salt–perfect for pairing with a drink. I couldn't stop reaching for them as I lounged in a comfy chair in my sundress, hair and skin salty and tanned from a day at the beach–I had to play the part, right? While this recipe isn't going to give you beachy vibes, it does make for a simple, bright dinner. If you have a skillet splatter screen, this would be a good time to use it (I don't, but I think they're pretty genius).

Serves 4

Salt

1 pound short pasta, like mezze rigatoni or penne

¼ cup olive oil, divided, plus more for the pasta

1 (15-ounce) can chickpeas, drained, rinsed, and patted dry

1 spoonful piménton (smoked paprika), plus more for garnish

⅓ to ½ cup store-bought or homemade pesto, to taste

1 lemon, halved

1 (4-ounce) ball mozzarella, torn into bite-size pieces

Handful of fresh basil leaves, gently torn (optional)

2 or 3 handfuls of baby arugula, or more as desired

Flaky sea salt

Red pepper flakes

Bring a large pot of well-salted water to a boil. Add the pasta, adjust the heat to maintain a gentle boil (no scary bubbles!), and cook just shy of al dente, about 3 minutes less than the package instructions. Reserve 1 cup pasta water, then drain.

While the water is coming to a boil and the pasta is cooking, in a 12-inch skillet, heat 1 snail circle of olive oil over medium-high heat until shimmering, tilting the pan so it's slick with oil. Add the chickpeas, season with a half-moon of salt and the paprika, and cook, stirring frequently so they don't pop out of the pot—toss them back in if they do!—until most are darker in color and mostly crispy, about 9 minutes (reduce the heat if they threaten to burn or are wildly jumping around in the pan). Remove from the heat and set aside to cool and finish cooking in the residual heat of the pan until the pasta is ready.

Return the pasta to the pot and set over low heat. Add ½ cup of the reserved pasta water and the pesto and toss to coat. Stir in more pasta water as needed if it looks dry, then squeeze in half the lemon juice and adjust the seasoning as needed with more pesto, lemon juice, or salt. Top with some of the chickpeas, the mozzarella, and the basil (if using).

Put some arugula in the bottom of each bowl, top with the pasta, and finish with a light sprinkle of paprika, flaky salt, and red pepper flakes, if desired. Add more chickpeas, if you like, and serve.

some thoughts: If you swap spinach for the arugula, it'll need more time to soften, so stir it in at the end with the pasta. Swap the mozzarella for creamy ricotta or even burrata, if you're feeling fancy.

skillet tortillas with eggs, labneh + greens

This is a comforting no-effort dinner that I love. I think just eating something warm makes me feel better sometimes, regardless of what I'm putting into it. It can be made a thousand ways, depending on what you have in your fridge and what you feel like eating. Sometimes I add a simple egg (page 13)—made in the same skillet after I toast the tortilla—and douse it with hot sauce. Other times I skip the egg and just add a ton of arugula/spinach and herbs, plus some pickled onions, or sometimes pickled jalapeños, or a little bit of pickled lime or achaar. The point being that this recipe is ready for you to make your own. I mostly love that the labneh melts a little bit and creates a creamy base for it all. Fold it up, tear at it; eat it however makes you happy.

Serves 1 or 2

1 or 2 tortillas (corn or flour or a combination; 4-inch corn or 6- to 8-inch flour)

Simple skillet egg (see page 13; optional)

1 or 2 spoonfuls labneh or thick full-fat yogurt, like Greek yogurt or skyr

1 or 2 handfuls of baby spinach or arugula

Sprig or two of cilantro or parsley, leaves and tender stems, gently torn

Extra-virgin olive oil

1 lemon or lime, halved

Flaky sea salt

Red pepper flakes (optional)

Have all your toppings and things handy, as this will all happen fast. Heat a dry 12-inch skillet over medium-high heat until very hot, about 2 minutes. Add the tortilla and cook until it starts to puff a bit, about a minute, then flip and cook until the other side is hot, about 1 minute more. This makes them soft and pliable, but if you'd like them to be more pizza-like and crunchy, then cook for 2 to 3 minutes on each side, flipping back and forth if they seem like they are browning too quickly. Transfer to a plate(s). Make the skillet egg in the same pan, if doing so.

While the egg is cooking, spoon the labneh into the center of the tortilla, spreading it out. Top with some greens, then the egg, herbs, a drizzle of olive oil, a squeeze of lemon or lime juice, some flaky salt, and red pepper flakes, if desired.

endless variations on this dish

scrambled eggs/pickled onions/jalapeño/hot sauce/achaar/leftover salad (weird but delicious)/leftover cooked vegetables/grated cheddar/grated Parmesan or crumbled feta/sliced avocado/cooked beans

simple skillet eggs

My friend Erica frantically texted me one day asking why her eggs stuck to the skillet no matter what she did. A New Yorker through and through, she had done her research and purchased a supposedly great skillet, and yet, stickage. I clacked back, "Add a splash of water to the skillet to loosen it up. You can also cover it if you want to finish cooking it over low heat."

An hour later: "It worked!! No more sticking!"

Adding a splash of water to the skillet helps loosen your eggs, and covering it so that it finishes steaming gives you that gooey yolk in the center—free of the icky white membrane-like film around the base of the yolk—without fear of overcooking it.

This easy egg recipe is more sunny-side up than a true "fried" egg, one that's super crinkly and wispy. Here, the whites are opaque without much crisping, kind of like if you had baked them in the oven. I tend to make these when I'm tired and want a built-in yolk sauce and something filling. Double or triple it if you need more than one egg, and later separate the whites with a spatula, as they will likely merge. It moves quickly, so timing is important to keep an eye on it.

Makes 1 egg

Oil, butter, or ghee

1 egg

Salt, freshly cracked black pepper, and whatever other spices you'd like

Heat a dry cast-iron or heavy-weight skillet with a lid over medium-high heat until hot, about 2 minutes. Add 1 circle of olive oil, tilting the skillet until the bottom is lightly coated with oil (we are not deep-frying here). Crack the egg into the skillet. Season the egg with salt, pepper, cumin, red pepper flakes, or whatever you like.

Cook until the edges and whites mostly firm up, about 1 minute and 15 seconds. Have the lid ready, then carefully, watching out for sputtering oil, add 1 spoonful of water to the pan and cover, tilting the pan to spread the water around. Lower the heat to medium-low, then cook until the egg white near the yolk is also firm and no longer gooey, 1 minute and 45 seconds to 2 minutes. The yolk might have a thin white cover, but I don't want you to worry that it's overcooked as it will still be runny. Uncover and use a firm spatula to remove the egg from the skillet.

sheet pan asparagus with tomatoes, eggs + feta

This is a recipe that I eat over and over again in the spring when asparagus pops up at the market, but since the formula is simple, you can swap in another quick-ish cooking vegetable like Broccolini. Baking the eggs on top of the vegetable creates an impromptu sauce when you break the yolk, but you can also flip them onto the hot sheet pan when you pull it out, if you like them over easy. Fresh or frozen corn would be a nice swap or add-on.

Serves 2 to 4, depending on how hungry you are

1 bunch asparagus, ends trimmed

1 pint grape tomatoes (you want them to be small or you'll need to halve them)

Olive oil

Salt

¼ spoonful ground cumin

¼ spoonful piménton (smoked paprika)

¼ spoonful red pepper flakes

2 or 3 (1-inch-thick) squares feta cheese (or add crumbled feta or grated Parmesan on top at the end)

2 to 4 eggs

Freshly cracked black pepper

Crusty or toasted bread, for serving

Heat the oven to 400°F. On a sheet pan, combine the asparagus and tomatoes. Drizzle 3 or 4 waves of olive oil over them and toss to coat. Season with a wave of salt, the cumin, paprika, and red pepper flakes. Toss to combine. Nestle in the feta squares (it's okay if they break apart) and poke the tomatoes with the tip of a sharp knife. Everything should look like it has a light sheen to it; if it doesn't, add a quick drizzle of oil until it does.

Bake for 10 minutes. Then remove and crack the eggs on top of the asparagus and return to the oven; cook until the tomato skins have started to burst and the egg whites are firm and don't jiggle when you shake the pan and start to brown at the edges, about 7 minutes more (eggs cracked directly onto the sheet pan will cook about 2 minutes faster). The other ingredients can hold up to more cooking time, so don't feel rushed if the eggs take longer. Finish with a grind or two of black pepper on the eggs, and serve with crusty bread.

scorched feta with corn + broccolini

I've binged *Sex and the City* many times, still shocked at how relevant the dating situations are despite some other outdated bits, as it makes great background noise while I'm cooking. I love the "Secret Single Behavior" episode, where the women share the weird, quirky things they do alone. This dish is one of my SSBs. I often eat this straight from the sheet pan, standing at my kitchen counter, scooping it up with bread and slightly burning my mouth on the hot, melty feta. Embarrassing, I know; I just hope my neighbors aren't watching me through the window and judging (they probably are).

Serves 2 (but can be doubled for 4)

½ (16-ounce) bag frozen corn kernels, or kernels cut from 2 ears corn

1 bunch Broccolini, ends trimmed, snipped into bite-size pieces

Olive oil

Salt

¼ spoonful ground cumin

Pinch or two of red pepper flakes

2 or 3 slices feta cheese, about 1 inch thick, or 2 ounces fresh mozzarella cheese, torn into bite-size pieces

Fresh cilantro, basil, or parsley, leaves and tender stems, gently torn (optional)

Pita or crusty bread, for serving

Heat the broiler with a rack 6 inches from the heat source. On a sheet pan, coat the corn and Broccolini with 2 waves of olive oil and season with a wave of salt, the cumin, and the red pepper flakes, then toss to combine. Nestle in the feta (these can be chunks rather than neat slices) and drizzle lightly with oil. Cook under the broiler until the corn and Broccolini have charred in some spots and the stalks are tender when pierced with a fork, tossing halfway but leaving the feta in place, about 7 minutes, depending on the strength of your broiler. Top with the herbs, if using.

Eat straight out of the pan with bread—no judgment—or however you'd like.

a simple cheesy pasta with lots of possibilities

This is your *I'm tired, it's late, give me some pasta* pasta. All you need is dried pasta, water, grated cheese, and a lemon, which might sound boring, but it's not, I promise. It's warm and satisfying, and it doesn't require you to think at all. It's also highly adaptable, so you'll find suggestions for ingredients to add at different stages—whether it's garlic, lemon zest or anchovies for the oil, or lemon to squeeze in at the end. Lots of these combinations are inspired by classic Italian dishes like midnight pasta, aglio e olio, or pasta al limone.

Serves 4 (or halve everything for 2)

Salt

1 pound dried pasta (shape of your choice)

Olive oil

Red pepper flakes

½ to ¾ cup grated Parmesan or Pecorino Romano, plus more as needed

1 lemon, halved

Flaky sea salt

Extra-virgin olive oil (your good stuff)

Freshly cracked black pepper

Bring a large pot of well-salted water to a boil. Take a spoonful, gently blow on it to cool it down, then taste to make sure it's seawater-level salty; adjust as needed. Add the pasta, adjust the heat to maintain a medium boil, and cook, stirring occasionally to make sure nothing is sticking to the bottom, until just shy of al dente, about 2 minutes less than the package instructions. Reserve 1 cup of the pasta water, then drain the pasta.

Wipe out the pot and set it over medium heat. Add 2 or 3 circles of olive oil, enough to generously coat the surface of the pan, then add red pepper flakes (use anywhere from a pinch up to ½ spoonful, depending on your heat preference) and heat until the oil is shimmering and the pepper flakes start crackling (this will happen quickly). Lower the heat to medium, then pour in the cooked pasta, ½ cup pasta water, and ½ cup of the Parmesan, and stir well until a creamy sauce forms, about 1 minute more. Add more water as needed to loosen it up if it looks dry or more cheese to tighten it if it looks too liquidy. Squeeze in half a lemon, then taste and add more lemon juice, cheese, or flaky salt as needed. Finish with a nice extra-virgin olive oil and a few grinds of black pepper.

endless variations

add to the oil: lemon zest/grated garlic/anchovies/sliced scallions/ tender parsley or cilantro stems, snipped

add a spoonful to the skillet after the lemon: labneh/strained yogurt/feta/ ricotta

add to the bowl: aleppo/sumac/paprika, urfa chili/harissa/calabrian chile paste/fresh herbs, gently torn

limey feta + sumac pasta

During a period of time when I struggled to sleep (hi, anxiety!), one of my yoga teachers mentioned in passing the technique of putting a little ghee in your nose before bed. Well, you can guess what I did that night. When my friend Nicole visited a short while later, we shared a bed, as friends do, and the next day, I realized she might have noticed the jar of ghee next to my bed, so I quickly explained. And, oh yeah, she had noticed, and the jokes were endless. This might be a you-had-to-be-there story, but it's all to say that I love ghee, whether for eating or sleeping.

Here, ghee is used for a smooth texture and richer flavor, but unsalted butter works, too. Sumac adds a bright, lemony flavor and textural element to the pasta profile, but you could swap it out for za'atar or Aleppo pepper. It's really the combination of ghee, lime juice, a drizzle of nice olive oil, and some salt that makes a luscious sauce.

Serves 2

Salt

½ pound long or short dried pasta

1 spoonful ghee or unsalted butter

Extra-virgin olive oil

1 lime, halved

½ spoonful ground sumac, plus more as needed

½ cup crumbled feta, or more as needed

¼ cup shelled roasted unsalted pistachios, chop them if you have the energy, or don't! (optional)

2 packed tablespoons fresh parsley, leaves and tender stems, gently torn

Flaky sea salt

Bring a large pot of well-salted water to a boil. Add the pasta, adjust the heat to maintain a medium boil, and cook, stirring occasionally to make sure nothing is sticking to the bottom, until al dente, about 2 minutes less than the package instructions. Scoop out ½ cup of the pasta water, then drain.

Return the pasta to the pot and set over medium heat. Add the ghee, 1 circle of olive oil, and the pasta water, stirring to combine. Squeeze in the lime juice and add the sumac, stirring until a smooth, glossy sauce has formed, about 2 minutes. Stir in the feta, letting it melt, about 1 minute more. Top with the pistachios, if using, the parsley, and some flaky salt.

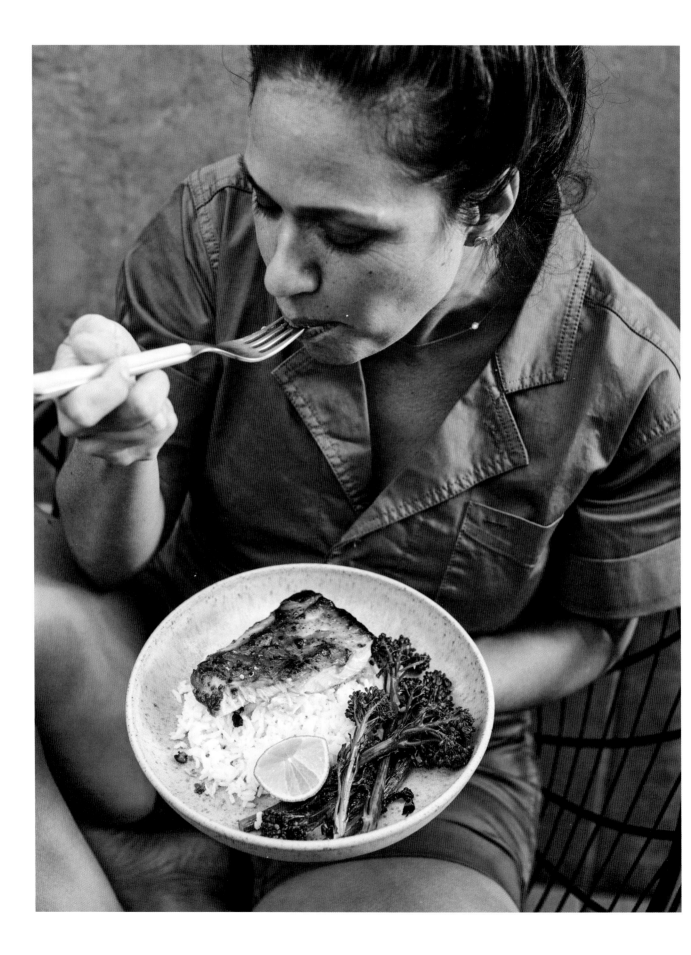

simply delicious miso salmon with broccolini (or asparagus)

Whether you've defrosted salmon the night before with ambitious plans that no longer seem within reach or picked up some on the way home, this recipe is perfect for low-energy success. If you'd like the top of the salmon even more bronzed, pop it under the broiler for 1 to 2 minutes at the end (this is nice for the Broccolini and asparagus, too); just make sure to turn the pan around halfway through if your broiler cooks unevenly.

Serves 4

2 spoonfuls white miso paste

3 spoonfuls grated Parmesan, plus more as needed

2 spoonfuls soy sauce

2 spoonfuls Dijon mustard

Olive oil

2 bunches Broccolini, ends trimmed

Salt

4 (4- to 6-ounce) salmon fillets, skin off or on (it will easily come off after cooking)

Red pepper flakes

1 lime, halved

Heat the oven to 400°F with a rack 6 inches from the broiler. In a large bowl, mash the miso, Parmesan, soy sauce, mustard, and 2 to 3 spoonfuls olive oil until a loose, smooth-ish light brown paste forms.

Add the Broccolini to the sheet pan, drizzle with 2 waves of olive oil, and season with 1 wave of salt. Toss to combine, rubbing the floret tips in the oil so they look slick. Add the salmon to the sheet pan, skin-side down, and rub the sides and tops with the miso mixture. Rub the floret tips in any remaining marinade in the bowl. Sprinkle everything lightly with red pepper flakes.

Cook until the salmon is just cooked through, depending on the thickness of the fillets, 12 minutes for 1-inch-thick fillets and closer to 17 minutes for thicker ones. If you want to place it under the broiler, then undercook by 2 minutes.

Squeeze half a lime over everything and serve with the remaining half, sprinkling Parmesan on the Broccolini, if desired.

pan con tomate with jamón

I love pan con tomate with jamón serrano or ibérico, a favorite dish of mine to eat in Spain, as it feels like two meals in one: I can pick off some of the striated-burgundy-and-white meat and also eat it on top of the garlicky tomato-rubbed bread. Making it at home is quite easy, as all you have to do is grate the tomatoes, and there's no actual cutting involved: Hold the tomato by the stem side, where the green bit is, then grate down until the grater gets too close for comfort (watch out for your knuckles!). A box grater is usually easiest, but you can use a microplane, too. The vinegar isn't traditional, but I think it helps a bit when tomatoes aren't at their peak.

Simple and satisfying, it's best served with a glass of wine. Well, the wine is optional, but it's just so nice that way.

Serves 2 as a meal or more for snacks

1 baguette, sliced into quarters then halved horizontally, or 4 to 6 thick slices country-style bread, toasted

2 large tomatoes

Flaky sea salt

Sherry vinegar (optional)

Extra-virgin olive oil

¼ pound jamón serrano or ibérico, or prosciutto

While you toast the bread, grate the tomatoes in a small or medium bowl, season lightly with salt, then taste and add a tiny splash of vinegar, if desired. Taste and adjust again as needed until it tastes good to you. Spread onto the hot bread. Drizzle with oil and finish with salt. Place the jamón on top and/or set out a snacking plate of jamón, too (let's be serious here, the stuff is delicious).

lime + pepper tuna (or salmon!) on toast

I have been eating tuna this way since my early twenties, as it's so easy and the addition of lime and pepper gives it a little kick so I feel like I'm eating something fresher than canned fish. The proliferation of high-quality tinned tuna, salmon, or whatever you like available in the States has greatly expanded over the years, so this will taste even better when you start with good-quality fish. While any kind of bread works for the toast, I love really dry crackers, whether it's a Wasa cracker or those crunchy dried mini toasts you can buy from European supermarkets. They are kind of bland, but with a little hidden sweetness that I find strangely addicting.

Topping it with some fresh herbs like parsley or cilantro and a healthy drizzle of high-quality olive oil is great, too. If you're using fish packed in oil, I would still shake off excess oil and taste before adding more, as a little bit of "fresh" oil can add some bright flavor notes to the dish. When making this solo, I use just one can.

Serves 2

2 (4-ounce) cans tuna or salmon in water or oil

1 lime, halved

½ small spoonful Dijon mustard (optional)

Flaky sea salt and freshly cracked black pepper

Extra-virgin olive oil

1 to 2 sprigs of cilantro, parsley, or basil, leaves and tender stems, gently torn (optional)

Any kind of bread you have or like, lightly toasted so it's firm, or crackers, for serving

In the bowl you plan to eat out of, add the tuna, squeeze in half of the lime, the mustard, if using, 3 or 4 grinds of black pepper, and mix to combine, breaking up the fish into large chunks. Top with a pinch of flaky salt, a drizzle of your nice olive oil, and fresh herbs, if desired. Adjust seasoning with more lime juice as needed. Spread on toasted bread or crackers.

hibachi-ish 5-minute shrimp

For many childhood birthdays, I had my party at Bisuteki Tokyo, a hibachi restaurant in Cambridge, Massachusetts. To this day, I am still a serious sucker for that shrimp. Whether or not the chef flips some shrimp tails into his pocket or his hat, it's all foreplay for this salty, quick-cooking shrimp to be scooted over and portioned out into my rice bowl. This sauce, while not quite the same as Bisuteki's, brings me back to those flavors, as there's a mustard-soy undertone and quick cooking under the broiler.

You can also heat up leftover rice on the same sheet pan or add bite-size pieces of baby bok choy, tossed in some olive oil, to cook along with it.

Serves 4

1 spoonful Dijon mustard

1 spoonful soy sauce

Pinch (or more!) of red pepper flakes

2 spoonfuls olive oil

1 pound medium to large shrimp, tails on or off (though off is admittedly easier to eat when you're this tired), patted dry

Scallions, snipped, for garnish (optional)

Cooked rice, for serving

Heat the broiler with a rack 6 inches from the heat source. On a sheet pan, use a wooden spoon or rubber spatula to mix together the mustard, soy sauce, red pepper flakes, and olive oil.

Add the shrimp, coating with the mixture, and spread out in an even layer and cook without flipping until the shrimp are pink all over with no gray spots, 4 to 5 minutes, depending on the size of the shrimp and strength of your broiler—keep a close eye on it. If you see halfway that the top is browning too quickly, then flip them over and return to the oven to finish cooking. Top with scallions, if desired, and serve with rice.

quick note about the shrimp: I find that "medium" and "large" are used pretty fast and loose when it comes to labels on frozen shrimp or shrimp from the fish counter in the grocery store, so look more for the visual cues, though the timing here works for both medium and large.

warm white bean + arugula salad with toasted bread chunks

I have this thing about eating greens when I'm hungover. I think I read in one of my college nutrition classes that drinking alcohol makes you lose vitamins and minerals, and eating greens is helpful for replenishing them (as is a Bloody Mary). The actual science of this, I have not investigated, but it's a living truth inside of me.

I first made this dish on a tired, hungover afternoon when I knew I needed to eat something green to make up for the damage I'd done but also really wanted to eat lots of bread. I tore up some crusty bread and toasted it in an oiled pan with a little bit of salt until crunchy, just enough to make me want to pluck a few pieces from the pan and pop them into my mouth, then warmed some white beans, dousing them and some arugula in a mustardy dressing and here you go. Good things can happen when you're hungover, who knew?! Please note that you can eat this when you're not hungover, too.

Serves 1 (or 2 with something else, like chicken, skillet egg, or so on)

Olive oil

2 slices thick, crusty bread or a bit less than ¼ of a classic French baguette, torn into bite-size pieces (about 1½ cups)

Salt

1 (15-ounce) can white beans, such as cannellini or navy, drained and rinsed

Red pepper flakes

Juice of 1 large lemon

1 small spoonful mustard

2 to 3 spoonfuls extra-virgin olive oil

2 or 3 generous handfuls of arugula

Drizzle 2 circles of olive oil into a large skillet and heat over medium-high heat until shimmering. Add the bread pieces and season with a full moon of salt, turning them over every minute or so, until they start to toast and brown in spots, about 4 minutes total. Add the beans, season lightly with ¼ circle of salt and a ¼ circle of red pepper flakes until warmed, about 2 minutes more, stirring occasionally. Remove from the heat and let cool slightly in the skillet.

In the bottom of a large serving bowl, mix the lemon juice, mustard, and olive oil until smooth. Taste and adjust as needed with more lemon, mustard, or salt. Pour in the bean-bread mixture, add the arugula, and toss until the leaves are coated with the dressing.

one-pot lemony miso + white bean chicken soup with spinach

This is a soup that starts you off thinking you're going one way—some calming Mediterranean vibes with the spices and herbs—then bam! Miso and soy give it a little bit of edge and depth. It's a soup that suddenly feels like it's been places, it's seen things, it *knows* things. If you taste as you go, which is typically a good choice, you'll notice that it tastes kind of blah up until the very end—that's when the deep flavor makers are stirred in—so patience, please. I'm terrible at that, but I'm asking you to trust me.

Serves 4

2 tablespoons olive oil

1 pound ground chicken or turkey, preferably dark meat

Salt

2 spoonfuls ground cumin

2 spoonfuls dried oregano

¼ spoonful red pepper flakes

2 (15-ounce) cans white beans, such as cannellini or navy, drained and rinsed

4 cups low-sodium vegetable broth or chicken broth (32 ounces)

Parmesan rind (optional)

1 heaping spoonful white miso paste

Soy sauce

1 (5-ounce) clamshell baby spinach or other quick-cooking greens

Juice of 1 medium lemon (about 2 tablespoons)

As much grated Parmesan cheese as you like

Heat the olive oil in a Dutch oven or large pot over medium-high heat until shimmering. Add the chicken, season with a half moon of the salt, cumin, oregano, and red pepper flakes, and cook, breaking up the meat into little crumbly bits and stirring occasionally, until browned in most spots, 4 to 6 minutes.

Add the beans, and stir to coat, then pour in the broth, add the Parmesan rind, if using, and raise the heat to maintain a simmer with small bubbles breaking across the surface of the liquid (bringing it to a raging boil will overcook the meat). Cook until starting to thicken, about 15 minutes.

Stir in the miso, a spoonful or two of soy sauce, and spinach, making sure to break the miso apart using a wooden spoon and press the beans against the wall of the pot, which will thicken the soup. Cook for about 5 minutes more, until the spinach is wilted and you can't spot any miso clumps. Squeeze in the lemon, stir, and add a hefty sprinkling of cheese, and season to taste with more soy sauce and/or cheese.

note: You can also swap ½ pound chicken or turkey sausage, removed from the casing, for the ground meat.

soy-steamed salmon fillets with greens

(tastier than it sounds, I promise)

"I'm an ideas man!" my brother-in-law, Robby, said when we started talking about toppings for this dish. He was throwing things out there and I was loving it. I was staying with Robby and my sister in LA when my sister cooked this lazy (but ingenious) way of making salmon with some steamed and crunchy greens served with rice. It's perfect for nights when you're tired but want something hearty and full of flavor. The salmon will be delicious and won't overcook, as it steams in a foil-covered pan, but the toppings are really what make the dinner fun and different every time.

Serves 2 to 4

1 bunch leafy greens, such as kale, chard, or collards, leaves stemmed and roughly torn into bite-size pieces

Olive oil

Salt

2 to 4 (4- to 6-ounce) salmon fillets, skin on or off

3 or 4 spoonfuls soy sauce

1 lemon or lime, halved

Heat the oven to 400°F. Add the greens to a sheet pan, drizzle with 2 waves of olive oil (or enough so lightly coated with a glistening sheen), and season with a wave of salt. Scrunch together with your hands, then spread out. Nestle the salmon skin-side down in the center of the pan, in between the greens, so it has direct contact with the pan; drizzle the tops with olive oil and a few spoonfuls of soy sauce. Tuck a lemon half in the corner. Cover tightly with foil and bake in the oven for 8 minutes to steam (salmon will be pink but not fully cooked through).

Remove the cover and cook until the salmon is done to your liking, 4 to 7 minutes more, depending on the thickness of the salmon, letting the greens crisp a little and the top of the salmon darken in color. (A thin fillet will be just cooked through at 4 minutes, while a thicker, 1- to 1½-inch-thick fillet will be cooked through at 7 minutes.)

Squeeze the cooked lemon half all over and serve with toppings of your choice and the remaining lemon, seasoning as

topping ideas: Squeeze some sriracha or Kewpie mayo, or sprinkle sesame seeds (or furikake, if you have it), on top of the salmon and greens. Some chopped scallions or cilantro would also be great. Chili crisp wouldn't be turned away, either.

tinned fish + red pepper + vinegary pasta

In Menorca, I played a game where I would pick two or three ingredients outside my typical realm of go-tos while food shopping to see what I could make out of them when I got home (this is what happens when you spend seven weeks by yourself on a small island). It's like that saying, "Do one thing a day that scares you," and it encouraged me to break my cooking patterns and be more creative, which worked out so that you didn't end up with a book full of feta, lemon, and cumin dishes (though there are a lot of those, too, let's be honest).

I've always shied away from jarred red peppers for some reason, but they are silky, flavorful, and a wonderful weeknight cooking tool—not sure what took me so long to get on board. The pickled peppers provide acidity, so don't worry too much about shaking them as you pick them out of the jar; we want some of that vinegary liquid to make its way into the pasta—you can even dribble in a little extra liquid at the end if you feel the flavor needs a little something else.

Serves 4 (can easily be halved for 2)

Salt

1 pound short dried pasta, such as fusilli, penne, cavatappi, or your favorite shape

Olive oil

1 (8-ounce) jar whole or sliced pickled guindilla peppers or pepperoncini

1 (8-ounce) jar sliced roasted red peppers, preferably in oil

Pimentón (smoked paprika)

1 (6- or 7-ounce) can or jar tuna or other tinned fish, such as salmon, trout, or sardines, packed in oil or water

1 or 2 spoonfuls Dijon mustard, depending on your preference

Freshly cracked black pepper

Small handful of fresh parsley or basil, leaves and tender stems, roughly torn or chopped (optional)

Bring a large pot of well-salted water to a boil. Add the pasta, adjust the heat to maintain a gentle boil, and cook, stirring occasionally to make sure nothing is sticking to the bottom, until just shy of al dente, about 2 minutes less than the package instructions. Scoop out 1 cup of the pasta water, then drain the pasta in a colander. Toss with olive oil in the colander and keep in the sink.

Wipe out the pan and set it over medium-high heat. Add 2 full circles of oil, tilting the pan to evenly coat, and heat until shimmering. Add the green and red peppers (they should look about even in terms of green and red color in the pan), then top with a light layer of paprika, like a dusting of snow that just barely covers the ground, and a half-moon of salt. Stir, then cook, undisturbed, until the green peppers start to blister, about 2 minutes.

Add the pasta, tuna, and a spoonful of mustard, then use the mustard spoon to add 2 spoonfuls of the reserved pasta water. Stir until the noodles look well coated. If dry, add more pasta water a spoonful at a time to loosen it. Taste and add more mustard or salt as needed.

Top with a generous amount of black pepper and herbs, if using, and a final drizzle of olive oil, if you feel like it.

endless variations on this dish
use crushed pitted green olives or drained capers for the peppers; leftover chicken or white beans for the tuna (add white beans with the peppers); red pepper flakes for the paprika

10-minute spicy tomato pasta

This is my go-to when I'm-super-tired-and-hungry/on-the-verge-of-getting-hangry dinner, as it relies on things I usually crave in this state and have on hand—tomato paste, harissa, and dried pasta. If I have some baby spinach or arugula lingering in the fridge, a handful or two also goes in. This recipe serves two people, but you can easily halve it or double it as needed.

Serves 2

Salt

½ pound pasta (I love short tubular shapes, but anything will work!)

Olive oil

2 heaping spoonfuls tomato paste, preferably double-concentrated

2 spoonfuls harissa

Spoonful of labneh or sprinkle of grated Parmesan (optional)

Bring a medium pot of generously salted water to a boil. Add the pasta, adjust the heat to maintain a medium boil (not the scary bubbles), and cook until al dente, 1 to 2 minutes less than the package instructions—make sure to bite into a noodle before pulling the pot off the heat. Scoop out a cup of pasta water, then drain.

About 5 minutes before the pasta is ready, heat 1 circle of olive oil in a 12-inch skillet over medium-high heat until shimmering, tilting the skillet so the bottom is slick with oil. Add the tomato paste and harissa, stirring to combine, and cook, stirring occasionally, until a deeper red color, 2 to 3 minutes.

Reduce the heat to low, then add the drained pasta to the skillet along with a few spoonfuls of water, stirring well to combine until all the noodles are an orange-red color. Add more water as needed so it's glossy looking. Stir in some labneh now, if using, or place in bowls and top with the cheese, if you'd like.

miso-ghee soba noodles

Miso and ghee are a match made in heaven, in my opinion, and this recipe takes advantage of that salty, aromatic combination with a hit of acidity to coat quick-cooking soba noodles. If you're tired of spinach, try adding wakame or ½ cup frozen vegetables like shelled edamame or corn to the noodles. Or cook other vegetables in the same way: melt ghee and miso; add bite-size pieces of broccoli, baby bok choy, or shredded Brussels sprouts; and cook until charred in spots and tender. Finish with a splash of soy sauce and squeeze of lime juice and eat it all together!

Serves 2

2 bundles dried soba noodles (about 6 ounces)

White miso paste

Ghee or unsalted butter

Soy sauce

1 lime, halved

¼ cup packed fresh cilantro, leaves and tender stems, gently torn (optional)

2 scallions, light green and white parts only, thinly snipped or sliced (optional)

Bring a medium pot of water to a boil. Add the soba, adjusting the heat to maintain a gentle simmer, and cook until just tender, according to the package instructions, 5 to 7 minutes, stirring occasionally to make sure nothing is sticking. Drain, then immediately run through with cold water, separating the noodles with your fingers to avoid gummy, mushy noodles. Shake the strainer to get rid of excess water.

Wipe out the same pot, then add the 1 spoonful of miso and 1 spoonful of ghee over medium heat, mixing constantly until the miso and ghee blend together. Immediately stir in the noodles and toss to combine and coat them. Season as needed with more miso or ghee, until the noodles have a nutty, buttery taste to them. Finish with a splash of soy sauce and squeeze half a lime over it. Taste, adding more soy or lime if needed. Transfer to bowls and top with the cilantro and scallions, if using.

lemony carbonara-ish pasta

I wouldn't dare call this a carbonara because purists would have my head, and rightly so, but *it is* inspired by that lush, egg-filled sauce. This version happens to not have any cheese. Not that you can't add cheese—you totally can sprinkle a little bit on top to up the flavor. If you're feeling energetic, zest the lemon, too, but if the idea of washing the Microplane fills you with dread, forget I said anything. You can also stir in some spinach for a little green or place some arugula in the bottom of your serving bowl and spoon the hot pasta on top to soften it.

Serves 2

Salt

½ pound short pasta (shape of your choosing)

2 eggs

1 lemon, halved

1 spoonful olive oil

2 or 3 handfuls of baby arugula or other delicate baby greens

Red pepper flakes and/or za'atar (optional)

Grated Parmesan, for garnish (optional)

Bring a large pot of well-salted water to a boil. Add the pasta, adjust the heat to maintain a gentle boil, and cook until al dente, about 2 minutes less than the package instructions.

Meanwhile, crack the eggs into a small bowl and use a fork to whisk together. Squeeze in the juice of ½ lemon, add the olive oil, season with a half-moon of salt, and gently beat again to combine.

Just before the pasta is done, slowly transfer 4 spoonfuls of pasta water to the egg mixture (add a bit more if some spilled during the travels), and whisk together until it becomes a softer, yellow color.

Drain the pasta, and return to the pot over low heat with the egg mixture, mixing well to combine and coat until a smooth, creamy sauce forms, it's almost looks mac-'n'-cheese-like, about 1 minute more. (Avoid putting it on high heat or it will scramble.)

Off heat, taste the pasta, then season as needed with more lemon or salt. Add the arugula to the pasta if you'd like it really wilted or add to the bottoms of the individual bowls and top with the pasta so the heat just cuts the rawness but it stays intact. Sprinkle the red pepper flakes and Parmesan, if using, on top before serving.

chicken thighs with chili crisp

When my friend Ian gifted me a jar of a new brand of chili crisp that he loved, I quickly became obsessed. Determined to see how many dishes I could make using this richly flavored, heat-filled condiment before I reached the bottom of the jar, I immediately made this simple chicken dinner with a kick. Serve it with Miso-Coconut Rice with Greens (page 48), plain rice, or greens you have on hand.

Serves 4

Olive oil

1 to 1½ pounds boneless, skinless chicken thighs, patted dry and cut into 2-inch pieces

Salt

1 spoonful soy sauce

2 or 3 spoonfuls chili crisp, or more as needed

Fresh cilantro, leaves and tender stems, gently torn (optional)

Scallions (optional)

Drizzle 1 full circle of oil in a large skillet over medium-high heat, tilting the skillet so that it has a light coating across the entire surface. Add the chicken pieces, season the top side with salt, and let cook without moving until they release from the pan and are browned on the bottom, 5 to 7 minutes. Flip, season the other side lightly with salt, and cook until no pink remains, about 5 or 6 minutes more (cut into the thickest piece of chicken to be sure). Remove from the heat, then add a spoonful of soy sauce to the pan, using a wooden spoon to stir it around and scrape off anything on the bottom. Add a splash more soy sauce, if you didn't quite get everything on the bottom.

Spoon the chili crisp over the chicken, bringing the jar to the table. Tear the cilantro over the bowl and snip some scallions over, too, if desired.

on seasoning your food

(mostly a chat about salt + pepper)

A friend once asked me, "When a recipe says, 'season with salt,' how much are you supposed to add?" I offered a long-winded answer, explaining the various ways you might want to season a dish, to which she responded, "So . . . there's no *real* amount."

She's right—there is no set amount—and I don't think she found my response particularly helpful, so I'm hoping I can redeem myself here. Seasoning your food throughout the cooking process is essential for many reasons, and seasoning as you go also helps you build flavor gradually (which is where other spices and ingredients come into play, too). The issue is, there are many kinds of salt with different levels of "saltiness," and there's a difference between industrial salt (like kosher and table) and artisanal salt. Rather than requiring you to purchase a certain kind of salt, I want you to learn to season with your preferred salt— the classic "I'm not going to tell you what to do," which annoyed me endlessly as a kid, so apologies in advance if I've annoyed you with this.

Seasoning is also a personal preference or a taste we've become used to, maybe because we picked up on our parents' or partner's salt

preference, and maybe it's something we don't even think about. The later steps in many recipes, including mine, ask you to season to taste or salt to taste, and while that's vague, it's intentionally so, rather than vague out of laziness, at least on my part. You'll also find that I often ask you to season with more lemon juice or vinegar first, before turning to salt, as that little bit of acid is often what is missing when food tastes underseasoned.

This direction also leaves room for the cook to stop, take a second, sample the food, think about how it actually tastes, and then season to their preference. I often find myself doing things out of habit without thinking about why I'm doing them, so if you're someone who automatically sprinkles salt on everything before tasting it, this might be a good opportunity to see if your food needs it. I find that sometimes I have to close my eyes to really taste something; it helps me focus better (even if it looks a bit odd).

So when I say "season with salt," I mean with a light touch, far less than any restaurant chef would encourage you to use. I grew up with a mother who is very sensitive to salt, so I've always erred on the cautious side of seasoning because I don't want her body to be unhappy with the food she's eating, and I'm likely the same way, as I can immediately feel and see my body's reaction when I've had too much salt (waking up puffy and swollen the next morning or even the same night). You'll also find that if recipes have "salty" ingredients, say, miso or soy sauce, I skip seasoning with salt or use a minimal amount. I know many chefs out there will balk at this, but I'm more concerned with how my body (and your body) feels and balancing that with good-tasting food than with "doing what's right." I really don't care too much what the rules say, though I do respect them.

But I'm not a salt hater, by any means! I value and appreciate good-quality salt and what it does for food and the body, and I absolutely love a good finishing salt, which adds that tiny bit of oomph to bring out the dish's best qualities, just like a squeeze of lemon does. I am fairly picky about the type of salt I use—I love Bitterman's sea salt as my cooking salt, which I got hooked on after interviewing Mark Bitterman and reading his cookbook *Salted*, many years ago. If you're ever interested in learning more about the ancient origins of salt, its production around the world, how to use it properly, and what to look for when buying it, his manifesto is the one to read.

Just as I encourage you to buy thoughtfully raised and grown meat, seafood, and other ingredients, purchasing and cooking with good-quality salt is a step that cannot be skipped as it's all connected. Finding well-made salt makes all the difference in terms of the quality of what you're putting in your body and feeding to those you love. Find a salt or salts you love and learn to cook with those, hopefully with a bit of care and intention, rather than out of habit.

a quick note on pepper

Someone once pointed out to me during a cooking class I was teaching that I rarely use pepper in my recipes. I reacted, as one does when called out, with "That's not true . . . is it?" She was totally right. Out of habit, I used to call for salt and pepper in every recipe, but when it's just me cooking for fun, I really only reach for pepper in a few cases: when I'm cooking with turmeric, as pepper activates the properties in it; when I'm finishing something that calls for pepper, like a crisp green salad or scrambled eggs; or sometimes to finish something sweet like raspberry or apricot jam with ricotta on toast, where the pepper offers a nice contrast. Pepper, unlike salt, isn't used to draw out flavor—it adds flavor, so I don't feel like it should be added without thought. Do I sound like a broken record yet?

41

toaster oven leftover rice with greens

As a kid, I was obsessed with our toaster oven. For a brief period, we had a surplus of Nutella-like hazelnut spread in the house—a much longer story than can be explained in the space I have here—and I took full advantage. I would rush home from school, toast a pita, and then make pita-and-Nutella sandwiches, letting the hazelnut spread melt into the hot bread. Ever since, I've only had loving thoughts about the toaster oven, especially the amazing ones they make today! Like a full-on mini oven that can do everything and cooks so fast. Cooking for one or two in that tiny oven is a time-saver. Anyway, this recipe came about on a tired night with a bunch of greens and some leftover rice, as the story goes for this chapter.

Serves 1 hungry person or 2 medium hungry people

½ to 1 cup cooked rice (or whatever you have)

1 cup packed stemmed kale leaves, torn into tiny pieces

Olive oil

Salt

Red pepper flakes

Grated Parmesan

1 lemon, halved

Heat your toaster oven (or oven) to 400°F (toaster ovens vary wildly, so this is definitely a watch-and-see recipe). On your toaster oven sheet pan, combine the rice and kale, and drizzle with 2 to 3 waves of olive oil so that when mixed, the rice has a light golden coating. I would be conservative at first, then add more as needed. Season with a wave of salt, red pepper flakes, and a light coating of cheese.

Cook in the toaster oven until the kale and rice are crispy, about 15 minutes, stirring once halfway through. Again, this might take more or less time, depending on your toaster oven. Squeeze half the lemon over everything, toss, then season to taste with more salt or lemon juice as needed and finish with any toppings you want or none at all.

endless topping variations
yogurt/pickled lime relish or chutney/fresh cilantro/kimchi/chili crisp/snipped scallions/crumbled feta (or chunks added onto the sheet pan)

side note: If you have frozen homemade or store-bought rice, use that for sure. Just make sure to stir every 5 minutes or so.

lap dinners

sausage meatballs with halloumi + tomatoes

This recipe was born on a trip to London, where I met my friend Patsy at the grocery store on a gorgeous summer day, cool and crisp with a lovely breeze and that lightness and happiness that hits a city like London when perfect weather arrives. Our plan was to pick up some ingredients we could throw together quickly so we could spend less time cooking and more time drinking bubbles on her patio and hanging out with her baby girl. This meal is very close to what we made. You can use any kind of sausage to make quick meatballs that won't overcook, but know that their fat content can vary greatly, so it can be better to cook a pork sausage on a separate sheet pan to keep things leaner (and also accommodate non-meat eaters). Eat it with bread or a simple arugula or green salad with an acidic dressing.

Serves 4

1 pint grape tomatoes or cherry tomatoes

Salt

¼ spoonful dried oregano

Olive oil

¾ pound bulk hot Italian-style sausage (chicken, turkey, or pork), or links, removed from its casings

1 (6-ounce) package Halloumi cheese, squeezed dry, torn or cut into ¼-inch-thick pieces (too thin, and they will get too melty)

2 or 3 handfuls of baby arugula or spinach (optional)

Heat the oven to 400°F. Add the tomatoes to the sheet pan, and season with a wave of salt, oregano, and 2 waves of olive oil. Use the tip of a sharp knife to poke holes in the tomatoes. Shape the sausage into 1-inch balls using your palms, if you have the energy, or pinch them into 1-inch chunks (either is great!) and add to the sheet pan, rolling them in the oil. Add the Halloumi to the spaces in between.

Cook until the sausage is browned and cooked through, the tomatoes are softened, and the Halloumi is soft, 20 to 25 minutes. Add the greens to the hot sheet pan right out of the oven and mix together to make it more salad-like, if using.

broccoli rabe + sausage with quick croutons + cheese

This is kind of like the classically delicious Italian dish of orecchiette with broccoli rabe, sausage, and Parmesan, but deconstructed and served with croutons instead of pasta. It's great when you want to hit those salty, cheesy, crunchy comfort notes with a bit of green thrown in so you can feel good about the whole thing. Broccoli rabe is on the more bitter side, so using a strong cheese like pecorino and some lemon helps cut it, but you can also use Parmesan or red wine vinegar. Some of the broccoli rabe will get tender and soft, some crispy, and all of it can hold up to additional heat if you want to cook it longer to get more color on the sausage. Or skip the sausage and keep it vegetarian (just load it up with cheese).

Serves 2

1 bunch broccoli rabe or kale

¼ classic French baguette, or 3 thick slices country-style bread, fresh or stale, torn into bite-size pieces (about 2 cups)

Olive oil

Salt

Red pepper flakes

¾ pound hot Italian-style sausage (pork, chicken, or turkey), removed from its casings

sherry vinegar

½ cup grated pecorino or Parmesan, plus more for serving

Heat the oven to 400°F. Trim the thick stems of the broccoli rabe with shears, then cut the remaining stems, with leaves and florets attached, in half, then place on the sheet pan. Add the bread to the sheet pan. Drizzle with 2 or 3 waves of olive oil. Season with a wave of salt and lightly with red pepper flakes. Toss to coat until everything has a light sheen to it, adding more oil as needed. Tear the sausage into bite-size chunks, scattering on top of the greens and bread. The size can vary slightly, and it's totally okay.

Cook until the sausage is browned and no longer pink inside (cut open to see), the bread crunchy, and the broccoli rabe tender (or the kale crispy), 15 to 18 minutes. Remove from the oven, then finish with 1 spoonful of vinegar and cheese and toss to coat. Taste and add more vinegar or cheese as needed.

note: The photo has the ends of the broccoli rabe in it, but they tend to get a bit stringy and difficult to eat, so it's best to remove them. Sorry about the confusion!

lap dinners

skillet tortellini with blistered tomatoes

This recipe almost got the boot to section 2, because I call for fresh tortellini (a gift to weeknight cooking), which, if you're dead tired, you're not going out to the store for, right? But you can easily use frozen tortellini in its place—just throw it in with the tomatoes so it has a few extra minutes to cook. It's a dish that's yours to play with—add some harissa with the tomato paste for heat, or even stir in a spoonful of labneh at the end to make it creamy.

Serves 1 very hungry person or 2 medium hungry people

Olive oil

1 pint cherry tomatoes or grape tomatoes or Campari tomatoes, halved

Salt

Red pepper flakes or dried oregano

2 heaping spoonfuls tomato paste, preferably double-concentrated

1 (8-ounce) package fresh or frozen tortellini (see headnote)

½ cup white wine, preferably what you're drinking

Fresh basil, leaves and tender stems, gently torn, for serving (optional)

Flaky sea salt

Grated Parmesan cheese, for garnish

Add 2 full circles of olive oil in a 12-inch skillet with a lid, over medium-high heat, and add the tomatoes. While the oil is heating, use this time to poke the tomatoes with the tip of a paring knife or cake tester. Season with salt and a pinch or two of red pepper flakes and/or dried oregano, if you're in the mood. Let cook, stirring occasionally, until they just start to burst and break down, about 5 minutes. Stir in the tomato paste, cooking until it becomes a fiery red color, about 1 minute, using a wooden spoon to gently press down on the tomatoes to help them break apart more.

Add the tortellini, stirring to coat, about 30 seconds. Pour in the white wine, stir, then cover, letting it bubble, and cook until the tortellini are done, about 4 minutes more (try one and see). Uncover; if it's too dry, then add a splash of water. If it's too watery, then let cook uncovered for another minute (or add some cheese). Top with the basil, flaky sea salt, and cheese.

miso-coconut rice with greens

Comfort in a bowl, this cozy dish will make your kitchen smell incredibly rich and fragrant. This accidentally vegan recipe uses miso and soy sauce for some depth and to cut through the richness of the coconut milk. You can keep it as is; top it with salmon, shredded chicken, or a simple skillet egg (see page 13); or add a little heat in the form of red pepper flakes or chili crisp. The texture of the rice is on the softer side, so if you'd like a little crunch, top it with snipped scallions, toasted sesame seeds, or toasted nori strips.

Serves 2 (can easily be doubled for 4)

1 cup basmati or jasmine
  rice

1 (13.5-ounce) can full-fat
  coconut milk

2 spoonfuls soy sauce

1 spoonful white miso paste

2 or 3 handfuls of baby
  spinach, or more as desired

1 lime, halved

1 or 2 sprigs cilantro or basil,
  leaves and tender stems
  (optional)

Pour the rice and coconut milk into a medium saucepan with a tight-fitting lid, then fill the coconut milk can one-quarter of the way (about ¼ cup) with room-temperature water and add it to the pan. Stir and cook over high heat until the liquid starts to bubble, breaking up any coconut milk clumps. Cover and reduce the heat to low; if you do peek, there should be small bubbles forming across the surface of the liquid, though try to limit how many times you open it, if you can. Cook until most of the liquid is gone and the rice is tender, 10 to 12 minutes more.

Remove from the heat. Use a wooden spoon or rubber spatula to stir in the soy sauce, miso, and spinach, trying to mash the miso a little, until the soy sauce looks like it has tinted the rice a light brown. Cover and let sit for 5 minutes. Stir again, checking to see if you see any clumps of miso lingering behind. Squeeze the juice of 1 lime into it, then season as needed with salt. Spoon into dishes and gently tear cilantro leaves and top, if using.

cheesy eggs-in-a-hole

Back when I was a cooking editor for a website, I ran a weekly recipe series composed of submissions from the other editors, and when one pitched "eggs-in-a-hole," I genuinely had no idea what she was talking about. Immediately looking it up, I was shocked that I had never had or made such an easy and admittedly genius recipe, as it wasn't something I grew up eating. Now, I make it all the time, and, while the proper adult move would be to use a small cup to carve out a hole in the bread, you can also behave like me and just pull some out with your fingers and immediately pop it into your mouth. Should you have more self-restraint than I do, then toast the pulled-out piece along with the bread in the pan. Eat it with a fork and knife or just tear into it and dip (I'm a fan of the latter).

Serves 1 (but can be made for more!)

1 thick slice rustic-style or country bread or halved baguette slice (make sure it can sit flat in the pan)

Olive oil, or 1 small spoonful ghee or unsalted butter

1 egg (make it a good one)

¼ cup grated Parmesan, pecorino, or cheddar, or more as desired

Flaky sea salt and freshly cracked black pepper

Red pepper flakes

Use a small pinch bowl or cup, about 2 inches in diameter (see the book's spine or page 111 for reference), to carve out a hole in the center of the bread.

Drizzle 1 circle of olive oil in a heavy skillet over medium-high heat and add the bread, using it to spread the oil around the pan until lightly toasted on both sides (you'll hear it start to crackle in the oil), about 2 minutes total, flipping halfway.

Flip the bread again, and lower the heat to medium. Crack the egg in the center, coating the surface of the bread with a generous sprinkle of cheese. Let sit for 3 minutes without moving, then flip, generously sprinkle again with cheese, and cook for 35 to 40 seconds more, letting the egg whites firm up. Top with flaky salt, a couple grinds of pepper, and some red pepper flakes, if desired.

lap dinners

chipotle + cumin black bean soup

A simple add-it-to-the-pot soup, this recipe uses chipotles in adobo (use leftovers to make Skillet Chicken with Peppers and Onions, page 164), along with tomato paste, cumin, and oregano, to build flavor, plus black beans that soften in the simmering liquid. You can also add some fresh-cut vegetables like carrots, squash, or sweet potatoes for more bulk, as it's on the lighter side of things, or toss in leftover vegetables to warm up at the end. If you happen to use a bit too much chipotle or find it too spicy, swirling in a bit of yogurt will help cool it down and add a nice touch of creaminess.

Serves 4

Olive oil

1 or 2 canned chipotle peppers in adobo sauce, depending on your heat preference, plus 1 small spoonful of sauce from the can

2 heaping spoonfuls tomato paste

1 spoonful ground cumin

1 spoonful dried oregano

2 (13.5-ounce) cans black beans, drained and rinsed

½ cup jasmine or basmati rice (optional)

4 cups low-sodium vegetable broth or water

Salt

1 lime, halved

Heat 2 circles of olive oil in a medium or large pot over medium-high heat until shimmering, add the chipotle(s) and adobo sauce, the tomato paste, cumin, and oregano and cook, stirring, until fragrant, about 1 minute, breaking up the chipotle with a wooden spoon as best you can.

Add the beans and rice, if using, coating them with the spice mixture, then add the broth and season with a full moon of salt. Raise the heat to bring the mixture to a boil (covering it can speed this up), then adjust the heat to maintain a simmer and cook uncovered until the watery flavor cooks off and the rice is tender, about 20 minutes. Squeeze in the lime juice, then adjust the seasoning again as needed. Top with whatever you like, or enjoy it plain.

endless topping variations

avocado; snipped scallions; cilantro; feta or other creamy white cheese; yogurt or sour cream

quickie tomato pasta soup + salad

Drifting away in Savasana at the end of yoga, I was on the precipice of reaching that deep relaxation I had worked so hard for and was craving, when this idea popped into my mind: I was going to use tomato paste as the base for a one-pot pasta, adding water after I cooked the paste (kind of like the 10-Minute Spicy Tomato Pasta (page 34), but it looked different in my head). Once the idea was planted, I could think of nothing else but running home to eat it immediately, like the weirdo that I am. Except, because I was tired and hungry, I didn't bother to measure the pasta or water and immediately saw that I had added way too much water. While my vision didn't come to fruition, I actually loved it as a soup and made it again a few days later. I like to sprinkle in some arugula for green at the end, so it feels like a pasta/soup/salad combo, which pretty much hits all my comfort and happy points. The recipe below is for four, but you can easily halve it.

Serves 4

Olive oil

1 (4 to 6-ounce) tube tomato paste, preferably double-concentrated

1 pound short dried pasta (any shape you like)

Salt

1 spoonful soy sauce

½ cup grated Parmesan, or more as needed

A couple of handfuls of baby arugula

Red pepper flakes

Drizzle 2 circles of olive oil into a large pot, tilting until the bottom is slick with oil, over medium-high heat. Squeeze in the entire tomato paste tube, using a wooden spoon to stir around. Cook, stirring occasionally, until the tomato paste has turned a fiery red color, 2 to 3 minutes. Add the pasta, stirring to coat, then add enough water to submerge all the noodles with about ½ inch of liquid above them.

Season with 1 full moon circle of salt and a spoonful of soy sauce. Raise the heat to bring the liquid to a boil (remembering that covering the pot speeds this up), then adjust to maintain a gentle boil, and cook uncovered, stirring occasionally to make sure nothing is sticking, until the pasta is tender and to your liking. When done, stir in the Parmesan and arugula and season with a pinch or a quarter circle of red pepper flakes. Season as needed with more cheese or salt.

coffee
table
dinners

2

i'm feeling good,
but let's not go crazy here

for times when you have a tiny bit of foresight, can make one trip to the grocery store, and will likely make this tonight, if not tomorrow

Whenever I visit my sister, I love opening her refrigerator, as it's beautifully organized with everything easy to find in its appropriate place. I always stand there for a few seconds too long, wondering, in amazement, *What would life be like if it made this much sense?* My fridge, as she will easily tell you, is a hot mess. I start off with good intentions, with designated areas for cheese, herbs, yogurt, and so on, but much like my closet, once it gets too full, I just start cramming things in (I have accepted that this is who I am as a person). Yet somehow, usually, I know how to find what I need in this organized chaos when it comes to cooking (more or less with getting dressed, too).

We all exist in this world in different ways, and no matter how our fridge is organized, we still have to get dinner on the table. So you can be any kind of fridge organizer, and you'll still be able to make these recipes. You don't need a deep, well-stocked pantry, professional-level knife skills, or a lot of time—this section is for nights when you have 30 to 45 minutes to get dinner on the table from start to finish and don't want to do any heavy lifting or organizing. So, yes, there are a ton of sheet pan recipes (and one-pot dishes, too).

I love a good sheet pan recipe. Putting a bunch of things on a sheet pan and letting the oven do the work for you is a true gift. Having one with a built-in side dish is even better. And maybe you serve it with a pot of rice or a salad or just throw in another sheet pan of vegetables to pair with it. Into that idea? Well, say hello and welcome to The Mighty Vegetable Chart (page 110)! (It's impossible for me to not picture broccoli in a Superman pose with a cape fluttering in the wind when I say or read those words.) You'll find a simple cheat sheet/reference chart for when you want to throw something else in the oven to roast alongside a sheet pan dinner or cook a quick side dish in a skillet.

You can use these vegetables to bulk up the recipes in this section, or any meal, really. The information is there for you when you need it. So scrounge around in your fridge, look for that jar of mustard or wedge of cheese—or easily pluck it from the exact place you left it last time (oh, how I envy you!)—and enjoy these recipes.

charred zucchini + scallion pasta with caramelized lemon

One of the homes I stayed in in Menorca was in the campo, a rural area outside the city where there were lots of homes and small farms. I loved walking along the dusty roads in the early morning, checking out the rows of vegetables and horses. The neighboring house had this highly enviable row of doughnut and yellow peach trees that made the expression "ripe for the picking" come to mind. I had to put my hands in my pockets to resist picking one every time I walked by. The house I stayed in had a beautiful lemon tree, along with a bunch of other fruit trees, so I'm not complaining, especially as I made this recipe after plucking two right off the tree and adding them to the pan just a short while later. What a gift!

Serves 4

Salt

¾ pound short tubular dried pasta, such as fusilli, ziti, or cavatappi (use the rest of the box for a solo pasta on page 34)

2 large or 3 medium zucchini or other summer squash, halved lengthwise, seeds scraped out, and cut into ½-inch-thick half-moons

1 lemon, halved: ½ left whole for squeezing, ½ cut into thin rounds, seeds poked out, and sliced into ¼-inch-thick matchsticks

3 scallions, sliced

2 tablespoons olive oil

¾ cup grated Parmesan cheese, or more as needed

Red pepper flakes (optional)

Bring a large pot of well-salted water to a boil. Add the pasta and cook until just shy of al dente, 2 to 3 minutes less than the package instructions. Reserve 1 cup of the pasta water. Drain the pasta.

While the pasta is cooking, heat a dry 12-inch cast-iron or other heavy skillet over medium-high heat until very hot, about 2 minutes. Add the zucchini to the dry pan and season lightly with salt. Spread into an even layer and cook, undisturbed, for 2 minutes, then use a spatula to flip over as many as you (you can even scoot some up to rest on the sides of the pan if it looks crowded). Cook again, undisturbed, for 2 minutes more, then flip as best you can, repeating at 2-minute increments until the zucchini is browned in spots, 6 to 8 minutes total. Add the sliced lemon and scallions and cook until softened, about 3 minutes more. Stir in the olive oil and season lightly with salt.

Lower the heat to medium. Add the cooked pasta, ½ cup of the reserved pasta water, and ¾ cup Parmesan, stirring well to form a creamy sauce, adding more water if the sauce looks too dry or more cheese if too watery looking. Remove from the heat, squeeze in the lemon half, and stir. Season to taste with salt and red pepper flakes, if desired.

sheet pan citrus-ginger chicken with stone fruits

For a long time, I was very anti-fruit-in-savory-foods, but I was wrong. There's something they add—maybe it's a sense of lightness, summery joy, or freshness with their inherent sweetness—that lifts up savory dishes like this one. Zippy ginger adds a bit of a kick, while honey encourages caramelization and browning on the chicken. It's a beautiful meal for company when you're sitting outside on a deck or balcony on warm summer nights (before the mosquitoes come and ruin it all) but also for a weeknight dinner, too. For this recipe, look for slightly firm stone fruit, as ones that are too ripe will become mushy. It works well for fruit that isn't quite as sweet as you want it to be—the ones that you don't want to eat solo. Serve with a light green salad or orzo tossed with lemon and olive oil for something heartier.

Serves 4

1 teaspoon ground cumin

½ teaspoon red pepper flakes

2 teaspoons grated fresh ginger (from a 2-inch piece)

2 teaspoons honey

1 medium orange, zested and cut into thin rounds

3 tablespoons olive oil, divided

2 to 2½ pounds bone-in, skin-on chicken thighs

Salt

4 or 5 plums or apricots, or 3 or 4 peaches or nectarines, quartered and pitted

¼ cup fresh mint or basil leaves, gently torn or chopped

½ cup crumbled feta

Heat the oven to 400°F. In a large bowl, combine the cumin, red pepper flakes, ginger, honey, orange zest, and 2 tablespoons olive oil. Pat the chicken dry then season all over with salt. Coat with the ginger mixture, sneaking some under the skin.

On a sheet pan, add the orange rounds and stone fruit, drizzle with the remaining olive oil, and lightly season with salt. Toss to coat and spread out around the pan. Add the chicken, skin-side up, to the sheet pan, nestling it between the fruit pieces and layering on the oranges, if necessary. Cook in the oven until the chicken skin is crispy and juices run clear when pierced with a fork, 40 to 45 minutes. Top with the mint, sprinkle the feta around the sheet pan, and serve.

team broiler

it's fast, easy + perfect for weeknights

Yaz, you've changed my life." I looked questioningly at my friend, wondering what in the world I could have done to receive such a life-affirming statement—was he sure he meant me?

It turns out, it was the broiler that had made the difference, not me. I'd simply turned him on to using it. With that said, I understand how the broiler can be intimidating and a bit scary, as it still sometimes scares me. (We are going for full honesty in this book.) Here are some notes on navigating your broiler to make your life easier in the kitchen.

In the UK, and likely other parts of the world, the broiler is called the grill, which not only is a more attractive name, but also helps give an indicator of how it's used. I like explaining it as an upside-down grill in that the heat source comes from directly overhead, much like a grill's heat source comes from directly below.

what it's good for Crisping chicken skin for a minute or two, quickly batch-cooking shrimp (see page 26), getting a grill-like char on vegetables, or anytime you want intense, direct heat on something. It also works for toasting a lot of bread slices—just flip them halfway (and keep an eye on them so they don't burn). And melting cheese!! Whether it's cheese added to the top of a pasta dish or on slices of bread, sticking it under the broiler gets it all bubbly and browned.

where to find it Some broilers are in a drawer below (or sometimes above) the oven's main cooking space, but most are located at the very top of that space. Open the door of yours and stick your head in to check (when it's not on, please). This is something that I frequently do when searching for apartments because (a) I like to see what I'm working with, and (b) I prefer for it not to be in a separate drawer. The reason for this is such: If your broiler is in the oven itself and you use it to say, toast some bread, roast some vegetables, or whatnot, you're already preheating your oven, which is great if you want to bake or roast something after. Second, if something is burning or cooking too quickly, I like the flexibility of being able to move it one rack lower to finish cooking. Or, worse comes to worst, if I need to finish cooking it in the oven, it's much faster to heat it to the temperature that I want. BUT if the broiler is 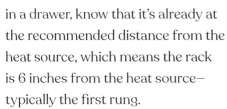 in a drawer, know that it's already at the recommended distance from the heat source, which means the rack is 6 inches from the heat source—typically the first rung.

know your broiler This is probably the most important thing. Not all broilers are the same: Some are powerful flamethrowers that will burn your food to a crisp in a minute or two; if you have a strong oven like that, then immediately go to the second rack. Other broilers are electric and will turn red hot when ready. It's good to know how strong yours is, but no matter what broiler you have, you need to keep an eye on whatever you're cooking. This isn't a case of setting it and forgetting it.

preheat your broiler For models with anything other than a flame, it's best to preheat it for 4 to 5 minutes to let it get fully hot. For stronger broilers that emit flames, I tend to find that they are usually ready to go right away, within a minute or so. I know I sound like a broken record, but it's good to get on good terms with your broiler.

the need to rotate Look at the surface of the food: Are some spots more charred than others? This means you'll likely need to rotate the pan or shift the food around so everything cooks evenly. This, though, can come in handy when you want to cook things at a lower heat—think of it as an indirect heat zone, kind of like on a grill.

sheet pan sumac + yogurt chicken thighs

Yaz, call me. I have something to tell you, read the text that popped up from my mom. Fearing the worst and assuming some sort of urgency, I immediately called her. "I have a recipe idea for you!" she said, and launched into this idea of combining sumac and tahini as a seasoning for chicken, which, in fairness, was a great idea. While I skipped the tahini, I loved the lemony flavor of sumac with yogurt, which coats the chicken thighs so they stay juicy and tender. This goes well with rice and a simple green salad, the sumac onions and parsley on page 68, or pita bread, yogurt, and some feta for little sandwiches.

Serves 4

2 tablespoons thick full-fat yogurt, such as Greek yogurt or skyr

2 tablespoons grated Parmesan

1 teaspoon ground sumac

1 teaspoon ground cumin

Salt

2 limes, zested and thinly sliced into rounds

2 tablespoons olive oil, divided

1½ pounds boneless, skinless chicken thighs, cut into 2-inch pieces

2 tablespoons packed fresh parsley, leaves and tender stems, gently torn or chopped

Heat the broiler with a rack 6 inches from the heat source.

In a large bowl, combine the yogurt, Parmesan, sumac, cumin, 1 teaspoon salt, the lime zest, and 1 tablespoon of the olive oil. Add the chicken to the bowl, coating it all over with the mixture. Set aside.

Arrange the lime rounds on a sheet pan and drizzle with the remaining olive oil, mixing to coat, and spread out. Add the chicken to the sheet pan. Broil until the top of the chicken is browned, 6 to 7 minutes. Turn the chicken over and broil until the other side starts to color and no pink remains in the center (cut into the largest pieces to check), 4 to 7 minutes more, depending on the strength of your broiler. If it looks like it's charring too quickly, then move the pan down one rack to finish cooking. Sprinkle the parsley on top and serve with the lime rounds, which you can eat.

farro salad with mozzarella, salami + sherry vinaigrette

For years, my go-to beach lunch was an Italian sub, particularly one from Faicco's Italian Specialties on Bleecker Street in NYC. The men who worked there, always ready with a quick compliment, made the process of buying a sandwich feel like a little ego boost. While I wouldn't dare try to re-create such a perfectly mastered creation as a Faicco's sub, this salad version is my tribute to it. Salty, garlicky, and filling, it can be served warm or at room temperature—perfect for taking to picnics, potlucks, or the beach.

Serves 4

Salt

1 cup farro, rinsed

2 tablespoons sherry vinegar

2 garlic cloves, grated or minced

½ teaspoon red pepper flakes

½ teaspoon dried oregano

2 teaspoons Dijon mustard

2 tablespoons olive oil

1 cup Castelvetrano olives, pitted, smashed, and roughly chopped

3 scallions, light green and white parts only, thinly sliced

½ cup packed fresh parsley, leaves and tender stems, roughly chopped

2 ounces salami, spicy or not, depending on your preference, rolled and sliced thinly

4 ounces cherry-size mozzarella balls or 1 small ball, torn into bite-size pieces, or 4 ounces Italian provolone (preferably Auricchio), diced

2 tablespoons drained and sliced peperoncini

Bring a large pot of heavily salted water to a boil. Add the farro, adjust the heat to maintain a gentle boil, and cook until the farro is tender and no longer chewy, about 30 minutes.

In the bottom of a large serving bowl, whisk together the sherry vinegar, garlic, red pepper flakes, oregano, mustard, and olive oil until smooth. Add the olives, scallions, and half the parsley to the dressing, toss to combine, and let sit until the farro is ready.

Drain the farro, add it to the dressing, and toss to coat, then stir in the salami, cheese, and peperoncini. Season to taste with salt (it might need a fair amount if you didn't salt the farro water enough), then top with the remaining parsley and serve.

how to smash olives: Use the flat side of your chef's knife (or the heel of your palm, in a pinch) to press down firmly on the olive so the meat splits and comes away from the pit, then pull off any meat still clinging to the pit.

smashed turkey burgers with sumac onions + parsley

One of my favorite things to order at a Persian restaurant is some type of kebab. The meat usually comes with a giant mound of yellow-hued rice in the center of the plate and plump tomatoes, their skin blackened from the grill, and served with sumac. The latter is usually in a shaker-style jar, the purple-tinted equivalent of dried oregano, Parmesan, or red pepper flakes at a pizza place, except this is generously sprinkled on the meat, lending its lemony flavor and coarse, salt-like texture. Here sumac is used both inside the turkey to flavor it and in the lightly pickled onion and parsley salad. You can always swap the onions for thinly sliced cucumbers, if you prefer.

Serves 4

1 small red onion, thinly sliced

4 teaspoons ground sumac, divided, plus more as needed for serving

3 limes, halved

Salt

¼ cup olive oil, divided, plus more as needed

1 bunch parsley, leaves and tender stems, roughly chopped

1 tablespoon ground cumin

1 teaspoon ground turmeric

½ teaspoon red pepper flakes

2 tablespoons thick full-fat yogurt, such as Greek yogurt or skyr, or labneh, plus more for serving

1 pound ground turkey, preferably dark meat

¾ cup crumbled feta cheese, divided

Toasted or warmed lavash or pita, for serving

In a small bowl, toss the onion with 2 teaspoons of the sumac, the juice from 2 limes, ¼ teaspoon salt, and 1 tablespoon of the olive oil. Mix in all the parsley. Set aside.

In a large bowl, combine the remaining 2 teaspoons sumac, the cumin, turmeric, red pepper flakes, yogurt, 1 teaspoon salt, and 1 tablespoon of the olive oil until a paste forms. Mix in the ground turkey and ½ cup of the feta until well combined, breaking up any lingering feta chunks. Divide the turkey mixture into 4 equal portions, then lightly oil or wet your palms so it won't stick to them and shape each portion into a loose ball.

Heat a dry 12-inch cast-iron or other heavy skillet over medium-high heat until very hot, about 2 minutes. Add the remaining 2 tablespoons oil, tilting the pan to coat until the surface is slick with oil. Add the 4 balls, spacing them out, then use a solid, sturdy flat spatula or the back of a wooden spoon to smash them until they are ½ inch thick. Cook, without moving, until a crust has formed on the bottoms, and they easily release from the pan, about 4 minutes. Flip using a spatula and cook until browned on the second side and cooked through, about 3 minutes more. Squeeze half a lime over them; cut the remaining half into wedges for serving.

Serve the burgers with the salad, remaining feta, bread, and lime wedges.

ginger-soy salmon cubes + broccolini

A dish that's far greater than the sum of its parts, you can serve these solo, on top of rice seasoned with a little bit of soy sauce and lime juice, or as part of a grain bowl. You'll want to source thick salmon fillets, likely center-cut, so you can achieve a nice cube shape. While I suggest Broccolini because I would eat it every day if I could, asparagus or kale would be great swaps. Your salmon cubes will likely be different shapes and sizes, given that's how salmon is shaped, so just know that smaller pieces are fine. These will get darker on the outside and more cooked—I love these variations—so you can let your dinner guests know to choose their cubes accordingly, depending on their doneness preference.

Serves 4

2 teaspoons grated fresh ginger (from a 2-inch piece)

2 tablespoons soy sauce

2 teaspoons honey

Red pepper flakes

1 bunch scallions, light green and white parts only, thinly sliced

1½ pounds skinless center-cut salmon pieces, cut into 1-inch cubes

1 bunch Broccolini, ends trimmed, halved lengthwise, or 1 small head broccoli, florets and tender stems cut into bite-size pieces

2 tablespoons olive oil

Salt

¼ cup fresh cilantro, leaves and tender stems, gently torn or chopped

1 lime, halved

Heat the oven to 400°F. In a large bowl, mix together the ginger, soy sauce, honey, red pepper flakes (use anywhere from a pinch up to ¼ teaspoon, depending on your heat preference), and scallions until combined. Add the salmon and toss to coat. On a sheet pan, toss the Broccolini with the olive oil and season lightly with salt, then spread it out on the pan. Cook for five minutes. Shake off any excess marinade from the salmon and arrange on the sheet pan between the pieces of Broccolini.

Return to the oven and cook until the salmon is just cooked through with a solid pink center and the Broccolini florets are crisp and stalks tender, 12 to 15 minutes. Top with the cilantro and squeeze ½ lime over everything, then cut the rest into wedges for serving.

garlicky ground chicken with ginger + scallions

Sometimes happy things happen when it all falls apart: This recipe is the result of exactly that. I was making Gingery Chicken Meatballs with Coconut Rice (see page 136), but they were too wet—I was using thawed frozen meat that just had too much liquid in it, which I knew as I was shaping them. I stubbornly continued even though I knew it was useless. Once a few fell apart during the cooking process, I uttered a good old-fashioned "F*** it!" and smashed the remaining balls into crumbly, almost larb-style bits. The result? Utterly delicious. I was obsessed, and decided to repeat it.

I ask you to make two big balls (though four would be great, too) so that the bottom gets that gorgeous, delicious crust and the inside kind of steams so it doesn't dry out, which can happen too often with ground chicken. Finally, in what I hope feels like a tremendous amount of fun, you get to break apart the balls to finish cooking. I'd eat this with sliced avocado on top, either over rice or in lettuce cups, and maybe with a dollop of yogurt.

Serves 4

3 scallions, sliced

1 jalapeño, seeded and diced

2 garlic cloves, grated or minced

About 2 teaspoons grated fresh ginger (from a 2-inch piece)

Salt

1 tablespoon soy sauce

2 tablespoons mayonnaise, preferably Kewpie

¾ cup packed fresh cilantro, leaves and tender stems, finely chopped, plus ¼ cup, gently torn, for garnish

1 pound ground chicken, preferably dark meat

2 tablespoons olive oil

1 lime, halved

Cooked rice, for serving

1 ripe Hass avocado, sliced, for serving (optional)

In a large bowl, combine the scallions, jalapeño, garlic, ginger, ½ teaspoon salt, the soy sauce, mayonnaise, and chopped cilantro. Gently mix in the ground chicken until it's more or less speckled with green without any large pink spots. Form the mixture into 2 loose, large balls.

Heat the olive oil in a 12-inch cast-iron skillet over medium-high heat until shimmering. Add the 2 balls and cook, without moving them, until the bottoms are browned, about 5 minutes. Use a wooden spoon to break apart the balls into small, crumbly pieces (enjoy this part!), spreading them out over the pan, then cook, stirring every minute or so, until no pink remains, 2 to 3 minutes more. Squeeze half a lime over everything, stirring to scrape up anything on the bottom of the pan. Cut the remaining lime half into wedges. Serve with the rice, avocado, if using, and lime wedges.

one-pot lemony cumin chicken with rice + feta

Emanating a sunny disposition with a little help from our friend turmeric, this dish is that bowl of comfort to turn to when you want something simple, flavorful, and warming. Turmeric is a strong and potent ingredient, one that can't easily be missed. A little too much can make a dish bitter, while just enough gives it a deep flavor and sun-like color. If you have cumin seeds, please use them, but I don't want you to rush out and buy them if this will be their only use.

Serves 4

Salt and freshly ground black pepper

1 teaspoon ground cumin

1 teaspoon dried oregano

½ teaspoon ground turmeric

½ teaspoon red pepper flakes

2 pounds boneless, skinless chicken thighs, cut into 2-inch pieces

2 tablespoons olive oil

1 teaspoon cumin seeds (optional)

1 cup basmati rice

2 lemons: 1 zested and juiced, 1 halved

½ cup crumbled feta, preferably Bulgarian

¼ cup packed fresh parsley or dill, roughly chopped

Yogurt, for serving

In a large bowl, combine 1 teaspoon salt, a few grinds of black pepper, the cumin, oregano, turmeric, and red pepper flakes. Pat the chicken dry, then coat with the spice mixture (it will be a light coating).

Heat the olive oil and cumin seeds, if using, in a Dutch oven or large pot with a tight-fitting lid over medium-high heat until sizzling (do not let them burn), 1 to 2 minutes. Add the chicken (it will be crowded, and that's okay) and cook until most pieces are white all over, about 5 minutes, stirring halfway.

Add the rice to the pan and toss to coat in the oil, about 30 seconds. Pour in 2 cups water, then add the lemon zest, lemon juice, and 1 teaspoon salt, spreading it all out in an even layer—not all the chicken will be submerged. Raise the heat to bring the liquid to a gentle boil with medium bubbles popping up, then immediately reduce the heat to low. Cover and cook at a gentle simmer until the rice is tender, most of the liquid has been absorbed, and there is no pink in the thickest piece of chicken (cut it open to see), 15 to 18 minutes more.

Remove from the heat, then squeeze in the juice from ½ lemon, stir in the feta, and adjust as needed with more salt or lemon juice. Top with the herbs and serve with the yogurt.

pesto pasta with broccolini + blistered tomatoes

This brilliant method—which is Italian in nature, but which I picked up from my cousin Leyla as she made it for her two boys—is great because it leaves the pasta water for you to use more if needed and doesn't waste flavorful liquid down the drain (or make you have to clean a strainer, which I oddly find stressful, as bits of food are forever clinging to it for dear life). The pasta will bring some of the water with it to the pan to make the sauce, so you only have to add a little extra if it looks dry. Everything in this dish will be soft and tender, which I find comforting; plus, it's ready in 15 minutes, which is fantastic for everyone.

Serves 4

Salt

1 pound long pasta, such as spaghetti, tagliatelle, or bucatini

2 bunches Broccolini, rough ends trimmed, florets and stems snipped into bite-size pieces, and thick pieces halved lengthwise

2 tablespoons olive oil, plus more for drizzling

1 pint cherry tomatoes or grape tomatoes (about 2 cups)

Red pepper flakes

3 to 4 tablespoons store-bought or homemade pesto, or more to taste

Bring a large pot of well-salted water to a boil. Add the pasta, adjust the heat to maintain a medium boil (big bubbles but not scary ones), and cook according to the package instructions until there is 5 minutes left in the cooking time. Then add the Broccolini and cook until the pasta and Broccolini are tender.

When the pasta goes into the pot, heat the olive oil and tomatoes in a 12-inch cast-iron or other heavy skillet over medium-high heat. Use the oil heating time to poke the tomatoes with the sharp tip of a paring knife or a cake tester to help them burst, stopping if/when the oil starts to splatter. Season with salt and red pepper flakes (use anywhere from a pinch up to ¼ teaspoon, depending on your heat preference). Cook, stirring occasionally, until the tomatoes start to burst and break apart, about 6 minutes more. Reduce the heat to low and cook, stirring occasionally, until the pasta is ready.

Use tongs to transfer the noodles and Broccolini, along with any liquid clinging to the noodles, to the pan with the tomatoes, leaving the pasta water in the pot. Raise the heat to medium and spoon in the pesto, then cook, scooping up the noodles and spinning them with the tongs so that they are coated by the pesto, 1 to 2 minutes more. If it looks dry, add 1 or 2 spoonfuls of the pasta water at a time. (This type of sauce will tighten once off the heat, so it's okay if it looks a touch liquidy in the pan. You just don't want it submerged in liquid.)

Portion into plates or bowls and top with a drizzle of olive oil.

quick tip: Loosen up leftovers with some water before heating them up and add a squeeze of lemon juice before eating.

skillet eggplant with orange, ginger + spinach

I made this dish over and over again in Menorca, and for a vegetarian dinner party I had there, as there was so much local citrus available. I love pairing the brightness and sweet acidity of orange with silky eggplant and the warming kick of ginger, which is sliced here. Sometimes I gnaw on the ginger because I love the way it tastes, but you can push it to the side. Sliced in large pieces, it adds a subtle taste to the overall dish; mince or grate it and add it along with the spices if you'd like a stronger ginger flavor.

Serves 2 generously

2 Italian eggplants, cut into ½- to 1-inch cubes

Salt

2 tablespoons olive oil

1 small orange, cut into thin rounds, then sliced into strips

1 (2-inch) piece fresh ginger, thinly sliced

½ teaspoon ground cumin

½ teaspoon red pepper flakes

2 tablespoons shelled roasted salted pistachios, roughly chopped

1 teaspoon soy sauce

2 to 3 cups baby spinach

¼ cup crumbled soft white cheese, such as feta or queso fresco

¼ cup packed fresh mint leaves or basil, or cilantro, leaves and tender stems, gently torn or chopped

Rice or bread, for serving

Heat a dry 12-inch skillet over medium-high heat until very hot, about 2 minutes. Add the eggplant to the dry skillet, season lightly with salt, then stir, spreading everything out in an even layer. Cook, undisturbed, for 2 minutes, then stir. Repeat, cooking and stirring at 2-minute intervals, until the eggplant is mostly browned all over, about 6 minutes more. Add the olive oil, orange, and ginger, season lightly with salt, and cook until the oranges are charred in spots, about 4 minutes more. Stir in the cumin, red pepper flakes, and pistachios, then cook, stirring, until fragrant, about 30 seconds more.

Add the soy sauce and let it cook off until you can't see the brown liquid bubbling in the bottom of the pan, 15 to 30 seconds, then lower the heat to medium and stir in the spinach. Cook until it just starts to wilt, 1 to 2 minutes more. Top with the cheese, sprinkle with the herbs, and serve with rice or bread.

braised chicken thighs with coconut milk, chile + pineapple

The pineapple addition to this recipe did not come about during a moment of culinary genius. Nor did it occur because I thought about how the sweet-sour profile often used in Thai cuisine might work here. It happened because I was too lazy to cut open a pineapple I'd purchased. After first making this, I knew it needed a little something more, which is when I looked over at my pineapple, the eyes on its body, fully yellow, mocking me with its obvious ripeness, countering my obvious laziness. That's when the lightbulb went off. Still, I hesitated because I remember all the bad '80s/early '90s food that contained overly sweet pineapple, but let me reassure you that the pineapple—just a cup of it—balances out the richness of the braising liquid.

Serves 4

1 (13.5-ounce) can coconut milk

1 tablespoon ground cumin

1 teaspoon ground turmeric

Freshly cracked black pepper

1 tablespoon soy sauce

1 (2-inch) piece fresh ginger, thinly sliced

2 to 2½ pounds bone-in, skin-on chicken thighs

Salt

2 tablespoons olive oil

1 (4 to 6-ounce) tube tomato paste (about ½ cup), preferably double-concentrated

1 cup fresh or thawed frozen pineapple chunks

2 limes: 1 halved, 1 cut into wedges

1 Fresno pepper, cut into rounds (and seeded, if you're sensitive to heat)

¼ cup packed fresh cilantro, leaves and tender stems, gently torn or chopped

Naan or cooked rice, for serving

Pour the coconut milk into a measuring cup or large bowl. Add the cumin, turmeric, a few grinds of black pepper, the soy sauce, and the ginger slices and stir to combine. Set aside.

Pat the chicken dry, then season all over with salt, including underneath the skin, if you're okay with that. Heat a 12-inch cast-iron skillet or Dutch oven over medium-high heat until very hot, about 2 minutes. Carefully pour in the olive oil, then add the chicken, skin-side down, and cook, without moving it, until the skin is browned and easily releases from the pan, 5 to 7 minutes (it's okay if the chicken thighs are snug in the pan). Use tongs to flip the chicken thighs, cook for 4 minutes more, then rest them along the sides of the pan, with the skin side visible to you, like they are fans at a stadium watching a soccer game in the middle of the pan.

Reduce the heat to medium. Add the tomato paste to the center of the pan and cook, stirring occasionally, until it's a fiery red color, about 2 minutes. Add the pineapple to the tomato paste and cook for 1 minute. Pour in the coconut mixture, stirring as best you can with the tomato paste, then nestle the chicken back in, skin-side up.

Raise the heat to bring the liquid to a gentle simmer, with small bubbles forming around the chicken pieces, avoiding a boil. Cook until the mixture has thickened and the chicken is cooked through, about 15 minutes. Squeeze the juice of 1 lime over the dish, then top with the Fresno pepper and cilantro and serve with the lime wedges and naan or rice.

caramelized onions + eggplant with tomato orzo

To achieve silky, sweet caramelized onions in the roughly 30 minutes it takes to cook this dish, this recipe uses a dry-pan cooking technique to force the moisture out of the onion (and also the eggplant, no need to salt them!)—you'll see it steam, which is pretty cool if we want to geek out about it. I like to set my phone timer and then dance around or clean up during the 2-minute waiting periods (the time goes by a lot slower than you think). Try serving this with an acidic salad, for both the green and to cut the full, rich flavor of the dish.

Serves 2 generously, or 4 with a side dish

1 yellow onion, thinly sliced (about 2 cups)

1 large or 2 small Italian eggplants (about 1½ pounds), cut into ½-inch cubes (3 cups)

Salt

1 cup orzo (about 8 ounces)

2 tablespoons olive oil

1 teaspoon dried oregano

¼ to ½ teaspoon red pepper flakes, depending on your heat preference, plus more for garnish

¼ cup tomato paste, preferably double-concentrated

¾ cup grated pecorino or Parmesan

2 tablespoons packed fresh parsley or basil, leaves and tender stems, roughly chopped

Heat a dry 12-inch cast-iron or other heavy skillet over medium-high heat until very hot, about 2 minutes. Add the onion and eggplant to the dry pan, season lightly with salt, and spread out in an even layer (it's okay for the pan to be crowded). Cook, uncovered and without stirring, for 2 minutes. Then stir, spread out, and cook undisturbed for 2 minutes more. Repeat until the onions have all softened in color and texture and shrunk slightly (and steamed excessively), about 8 minutes more. Lower the heat if the onions threaten to burn, though a little color is fine.

When the above steps are almost done, bring a large pot of well-salted water to a boil. Add the orzo, adjust the heat to maintain a gentle boil, and cook until tender, 7 to 9 minutes. Reserve 1 cup of the pasta water, then drain the orzo, drizzle with olive oil, and toss to coat. Leave the colander in the sink until the onions and eggplant are done in the steps below.

Lower the heat under the skillet to medium, add the 2 tablespoons of olive oil, and season lightly with salt. Cook, stirring every minute or so, until the onions and eggplant are silky and creamy, 10 to 12 minutes more, depending on the size of your onions (larger ones will take longer). Stir in the oregano, red pepper flakes, and tomato paste, scraping up anything stuck to the bottom, and cook until the tomato paste deepens in color, about 2 minutes more.

Reduce the heat to low. Add the orzo to the onions, along with ¾ cup of the reserved pasta water and the pecorino, stirring well to combine until a creamy, cheesy and pinky-red sauce forms. Add more pasta water if it looks dry. Finish with the red pepper flakes and herbs.

miso-ginger chicken thighs

We have a bit of dealer's choice here in the amount of miso used: I like the subtle flavor of 1 tablespoon, but some tasters preferred 2 tablespoons for an even stronger miso flavor on the chicken skin. I would try it first as is, then add more, depending on your salt and miso preference. This dish is meant to be eaten with another sheet pan full of vegetables thrown in at the same time; baby bok choy with some garlic and a finish of soy sauce would shine here, but Broccolini or kale would be great, too. Check page 110 for cooking times. Some cooked rice would also be nice.

Serves 4 to 6

2½ to 3 pounds bone-in, skin-on chicken thighs

2 tablespoons olive oil, divided

Salt

1 to 2 tablespoons white miso paste, depending on preference

1 tablespoon ghee or unsalted butter, at room temperature

1 tablespoon grated fresh ginger (from a 3-inch piece)

1 lime, halved

2 tablespoons packed fresh cilantro, leaves and tender stems, gently torn or chopped

Heat the oven to 400°F with a rack 6 inches from the broiler heat source. Pat the chicken dry, then coat with 1 tablespoon of the oil and sprinkle lightly all over with salt (remember, miso is salty). Set on a sheet pan. In a small bowl, mash together the miso, ghee, and ginger until combined. Rub the chicken all over with the miso mixture, sneaking some under the skin. Bake skin-side up until the skin is crispy and the chicken is cooked through, about 40 minutes. If the skin is not quite as crispy as you'd like, then place under the broiler for 1 to 2 minutes.

Squeeze half a lime over the chicken and top with the cilantro. Slice the remaining lime into wedges for serving.

coconut-braised salmon with vegetables

It was a hit with non-salmon eaters! my friend Joni texted after testing this recipe for me and sharing some with her neighbor, who is not a fish person. The bold, rich, and warming flavors of the saucy dish make it a great meal for salmon skeptics (or lovers!) in your life, as the ingredients and flavors all shine, rather than making salmon the star of the show, so it is a good way to nudge people into the fish world. As you'll see, you can use the vegetables of your choice, depending on what you have in your fridge or freezer, but serving with rice or pita bread for the liquid is nonnegotiable.

Serves 4

1 (13.5-ounce) can full-fat coconut milk

2 tablespoons soy sauce

1 tablespoon white miso paste

Zest and juice of 2 limes

1 teaspoon grated fresh ginger from a (3-inch) piece fresh ginger, the rest thinly sliced after grating

2 cups vegetable of your choice (about 10 ounces), such as broccoli florets, frozen corn, frozen peas, fresh snow peas, sliced bok choy, snap peas, or any combination of these

2 cups packed baby spinach

4 (4- to 6-ounce) salmon fillets, skin on or off

Salt

¼ teaspoon red pepper flakes

2 scallions, light green and white parts only, sliced

¼ cup fresh cilantro, leaves and tender stems, gently torn

Cooked rice or pita, for serving

Heat the oven to 400°F. In a 9 by 13-inch baking dish, stir together the coconut milk, soy sauce, miso, and lime zest and juice until combined, mashing and breaking up the miso and coconut clumps. Add the ginger slices, vegetable of your choice, and spinach, mixing to coat in the liquid. Season the salmon all over with salt, the grated ginger, and the red pepper flakes, then turn to coat in the coconut mixture and set skin-side down, spooning a little of the liquid on top. Scatter half the scallions on top.

Cover with foil and bake until the salmon is just cooked through in the center, 25 minutes for 1½-inch thick pieces (22 to 23 minutes for thinner cuts). Carefully remove the foil as it will be hot, then top with the cilantro and remaining scallions. Serve with rice or pita bread.

family-style dijon chicken with mushrooms

My cousin Leyla was clear about what this recipe should be named, as she wanted to be clear that it's kid-friendly. She was visiting me in Miami, and it was wonderful to have a real-time taster giving me feedback, especially one who doesn't hold back (we are very close). The chicken thighs have a slight French-bistro feel to them, with the mustard and vinegar, and pair well with the roasted mushrooms and silky onion wedges. Eat it with rice or bread for sopping up any pan juices.

Serves 4

1 tablespoon Dijon mustard

1 tablespoon sherry vinegar or balsamic vinegar

1 tablespoon soy sauce

½ teaspoon dried oregano

¼ to ½ teaspoon red pepper flakes, depending on heat preference

3 garlic cloves, grated or minced, plus the remaining head of garlic, separated into cloves, left whole in their skins (this extra garlic is optional)

3 tablespoons olive oil, divided

2 pounds bone-in, skin-on chicken thighs

Salt

1 red onion, cut into 2-inch pieces

1 pound cremini mushrooms, woody stems removed, larger ones halved

¼ cup fresh parsley, leaves and tender stems, gently chopped or torn

Grated Parmesan, for garnish

Heat the oven to 400°F. In a small bowl, combine the mustard, vinegar, soy sauce, oregano, red pepper flakes, grated garlic, and 1 tablespoon of the olive oil until combined. Pat the chicken thighs dry, lightly salt all over, then coat all over with the mustard mixture, including under the skin.

In a shallow baking dish or sheet pan, toss the onion, unpeeled garlic cloves, if using, mushrooms, and remaining 2 tablespoons olive oil, season lightly with salt, and spread out. Nestle the chicken thighs skin-side up between the onions and mushrooms. Rub any remaining marinade (there will be very little) on the mushrooms. Roast until the chicken juices run clear when pierced with a fork and the skin crispy, about 40 minutes. Sprinkle the parsley and Parmesan over everything, and serve more cheese at the table.

kale pasta with sausage + parmesan

This recipe is simple cooking at its best—and perfect for a weeknight dinner when you want something filling and comforting with a little bit of green in there. The greens are finished with a bit of soy sauce to give the dish more flavor than you'd suspect possible in this short amount of time. While the sausage adds both flavor and a bit of fat, you can also swap it out for white beans to make this vegetarian.

Serves 4

Salt

1 pound short tubular pasta (to catch the sausage bits)

2 tablespoons olive oil, plus more as needed

¾ pound Italian-style sausage (pork, turkey, or chicken), removed from its casings

1 medium bunch lacinato or curly kale, leaves stemmed and cut into 1-inch-wide ribbons (about 3 packed cups)

½ teaspoon ground cumin

¼ to ½ teaspoon red pepper flakes, depending on your heat preference

2 teaspoons soy sauce

¾ cup grated Parmesan

Juice of 1 lemon

Bring a large pot of well-salted water to a boil. Add the pasta and cook until just shy of al dente, about 2 minutes less than the package instructions. Reserve 1 cup of the pasta water, then drain in a colander in the sink.

Heat the olive oil in a 12-inch skillet over medium-high heat until shimmering. Add the sausage and cook without moving so it can brown, for a minute, then break it up into tiny pieces and cook, stirring every minute or two, until crumbled, browned, and crispy, 7 to 9 minutes. Add the kale, season lightly with salt, the cumin, and the red pepper flakes, and cook, stirring occasionally, until the leaves have started to wilt, about 2 minutes. Add the soy sauce and stir until it evaporates, about 30 seconds more.

Add the pasta to the kale mixture and stir in ¾ cup of the reserved pasta water and the cheese. Cook, stirring vigorously and scraping up anything from the bottom of the pot, until a smooth sauce forms with just a tiny bit of liquid pooling at the bottom, 1 to 2 minutes more. Add a splash more pasta water if it looks dry. Stir in the lemon juice, then season as needed with salt.

harissa-citrus sheet pan chicken thighs with kale chips

There are times when I make a recipe and think, *Oooh, people are going to love this!* And then . . . they don't. I mean, not that they don't love the recipe itself if they make it, but something about the title or whatnot doesn't attract them to make it. So I really hope you make this recipe, as this sweet, spicy, and earthy marinade works so well with chicken. Definitely marinate overnight or an hour ahead if you have the foresight. The kale chips are easy, crunchy, and delicious; they're fantastic on their own, and also play well with the citrusy notes in this dressing—both in the bits of caramelized citrus wedges and the crispy chicken skin.

Serves 4

2 teaspoons harissa

2 teaspoons honey

1 teaspoon ground cumin, divided

1 lime, zested and halved

¼ cup thick full-fat yogurt, such as Greek yogurt or skyr

2 to 2½ pounds bone-in, skin-on chicken thighs

Salt

1 red onion, cut into 1-inch-thick wedges

1 small navel orange, or 2 clementines or mandarins, cut into thin rounds and any seeds poked out

2 tablespoons olive oil, divided

1 small bunch lacinato or curly kale, stemmed and leaves roughly chopped or torn into 1-inch pieces (2 to 3 packed cups)

1 lime, cut in half

Heat the oven to 400°F. In a large bowl, stir together the harissa, honey, ½ teaspoon of the cumin, the lime zest, and the yogurt until smooth. Season the chicken all over with salt, then add it to the yogurt mixture, turning it to coat all over, lifting up the skin to sneak some under there, too.

Arrange the onion and orange rounds on a sheet pan, drizzle with 1 tablespoon of the olive oil, season lightly with salt, and spread out into an even layer. Shake any excess marinade off the chicken, then add it to the sheet pan, skin-side up. Roast for 30 minutes.

Meanwhile, toss the kale with the remaining cumin and olive oil and season lightly with salt. Remove the pan from the oven, scatter the kale over everything, and cook until the chicken has a nice crisp coloring, the juices run clear when pierced with a fork, and the kale is crispy, 15 to 20 minutes more. Squeeze half the lime over everything, then cut the remaining lime into wedges for serving.

kale, ginger + turmeric noodle soup

This soup is composed of all the things that I think are good for me when I'm feeling under the weather, namely ginger, turmeric, and lemon. One chilly evening, I threw them all together in a pot with a leftover Parmesan rind and topped it with some homemade croutons. The Parmesan rind gives the broth a rich flavor and depth, but you can mix in grated cheese to achieve that same end result. If you have leftover roasted vegetables—say, broccoli, Broccolini, or sweet potatoes—you can add those at the end in lieu of the carrots, which are optional if you don't feel like cutting them.

Serves 2

2 tablespoons olive oil

1 small red onion or shallot, minced

1 carrot, unpeeled, cut into rounds

Salt

3 garlic cloves: 1 smashed, 2 grated or minced

2 teaspoons ground turmeric

2 teaspoons ground cumin

¼ to ½ teaspoon red pepper flakes, depending on your heat preference

1 (32-ounce) can low-sodium vegetable broth (4 cups)

Parmesan rind, or ½ cup grated Parmesan

1 (2-inch) piece fresh ginger, thinly sliced

8 ounces dried angel hair pasta

1 small bunch kale, leaves stemmed and torn into 1-inch pieces (2 to 3 packed cups)

1 lemon, halved

Croutons (see page 205; optional)

Heat the olive oil in a large pot or Dutch oven over medium heat until shimmering. Add the onion and carrot, season with salt, and cook until the onion begins to soften and the carrot becomes brighter in color, 4 to 5 minutes. Stir in all the garlic, turmeric, cumin, and red pepper flakes and cook until fragrant, about 1 minute. Add the broth, 1 cup water, the Parmesan rind, and the ginger, raise the heat to bring to a gentle boil, then reduce the heat to maintain an active simmer. Season to taste with salt and cook to allow the flavors to blend, about 5 minutes.

Stir in the angel hair and the kale and cook until the pasta and kale are tender, about 5 minutes. Stir in the cheese, if not using a Parmesan rind. Squeeze in half the lemon, then season as needed with salt or more lemon juice. Serve with some croutons on top, if desired.

whitefish salad

Wandering around the Union Square Greenmarket one day, I saw some gorgeous smoked whitefish and bought it without thinking what I was going to do with it. This mash-up is the result of what I had in my fridge, and while it probably isn't for everyone or an everyday dish, should you find yourself with some smoked whitefish or trout and no plan in sight, I hope this serves you well. It's a bit of a twist on a more traditional whitefish salad, not what you'd find in a New York deli. It gets better the longer it sits, so make it the night before or snack on it all week.

Serves 4

1 cup thick full-fat yogurt, such as Greek yogurt or skyr

½ cup fresh dill, leaves and tender stems, roughly chopped

½ cup fresh parsley, leaves and tender stems, roughly chopped

½ jalapeño, seeded and minced

½ small red onion, diced (about ¼ cup)

3 limes: 2 zested and juiced, 1 cut into wedges

10 to 12 ounces smoked whitefish or trout, skin and bones removed, flaked

Salt and freshly cracked black pepper

Toasted rye, sourdough, or crackers, for serving

In a serving bowl, mix together the yogurt, most of the dill and parsley, reserving some of the herbs for garnish, along with the jalapeño, onion, and lime zest and juice. Add the fish and mix well. Let sit in the fridge for at least 15 minutes. Season as needed with salt, then top with the reserved herbs and generously season with black pepper. Serve with bread and the lime wedges alongside.

crispy + crunchy oregano chicken

When I was growing up, my family ate dinner together every night, which might be one reason my sister and I both work in food today—we have so many happy memories of being around the dinner table. While my mom cooked, my parents would have *Wheel of Fortune* on, likely to keep us quiet, with the added lure of getting five dollars if we guessed the answer before the contestants. This chicken dish, which we called "chicken with greens," came out of the oven with salty and impossibly crispy skin. While my mom made it with Cornish hens, chicken thighs make an easy stand-in and go well with rice, roasted potatoes (see page 114), and some yogurt. Though a green salad or any other roasted vegetable (see pages 113–115) would also be nice.

Serves 4

1 tablespoon olive oil, plus more for the chicken

2½ to 3 pounds bone-in, skin-on chicken thighs

Salt

1 tablespoon dried oregano, plus more as needed

¼ teaspoon red pepper flakes

Freshly cracked black pepper

Roast potatoes, yogurt, and/or rice, for serving

Heat the oven to 400°F. Coat a sheet pan with the olive oil, tilting or rubbing it until it's slick with oil. Pat the chicken really, really dry, maybe once more after you think you've done enough. Season well all over with salt, including under the skin. Place skin-side up on the prepared sheet pan. Drizzle the tops with a little olive oil, then divide the oregano and red pepper flakes over the chicken skin, along with a few grinds of black pepper, patting the spices in so that it's mostly green with specks of black, white, and red (add a touch more salt, if needed).

Cook until the chicken skin is crispy and the juices run clear when pierced with a fork, about 40 minutes. Serve with the roast potatoes, yogurt, and/or rice.

spanish-style olive oil–poached fish with chickpeas

Fish is always a risky one to serve guests, I find, because there's a lot of room for error, much more than with a roast chicken or vegetables, say. Once overcooked, it's beyond saving, unfortunately, but this simple technique takes that worry right out of the picture. Plus, it has a gorgeous presentation with the paprika-and-turmeric-tinted cooking liquid. Simple enough for a weeknight and pretty enough for a party.

A thicker white-fleshed fish, such as halibut or cod, is nicer here, and it will flake apart slightly, which is totally fine (and I think looks even prettier). This dish is best served at the table, spooned into shallow bowls with lightly oiled and toasted bread for dipping. If you like, you can also chop up a preserved lemon and add it to the poaching liquid, too. Or sauté some chorizo in a pan until browned, then add it to the fish to give it a more salty, meaty flavor and color contrast.

Serves 4

Salt

1 teaspoon piménton (smoked paprika)

½ teaspoon ground turmeric

½ teaspoon dried oregano

½ teaspoon red pepper flakes

Freshly cracked black pepper

3 garlic cloves, grated or minced

Zest and juice of 2 limes

½ cup olive oil

1 to 1½ pounds skinless firm white-fleshed fish, such as flounder, halibut, or cod

1 (15-ounce) can chickpeas, drained and rinsed

¼ cup fresh parsley, leaves and tender stems, gently torn or roughly chopped

1 or 2 lemons, halved or cut into wedges, for serving (optional)

Heat the oven to 400°F. In a shallow 9 by 13-inch baking dish or a braising dish with a tight-fitting lid, combine 1 teaspoon salt, the paprika, turmeric, oregano, red pepper flakes, a few grinds of black pepper, the garlic, lime zest, lime juice, and olive oil. Add the fish and chickpeas, turning to coat everything in the liquid. Set the fish skin-side down.

Cover with foil or the dish's lid and roast until the fish is tender, flaky, and just cooked through, 20 to 25 minutes, depending on the thickness of the fish (at 1½-inch thick, it will take closer to 25 minutes). Remove the foil carefully (the steam will be hot) and finish with some black pepper and the parsley.

smashed ginger-scallion chicken burgers

SO GOOD—Mom clapped. Philip said he had "nothing to add, ready to publish." Some notes from my dear friend Joanna and her family when they tested this recipe for me. This makes my heart swell, so I hope you enjoy these burgers just as much as they did. Gingery, chock-full of herbs and crunchy bits of scallions, these burgers are great with a simple salad, eaten with lettuce or on a bun. There is no salt called for in the burger, as both miso and soy sauce cover that territory, in case you're wondering where it is.

Serves 4

½ cup plus 2 tablespoons thick full-fat yogurt, such as Greek yogurt or skyr, divided

1 tablespoon plus ½ teaspoon white miso paste

2 limes, halved

Salt

1 tablespoon soy sauce

2 teaspoons grated fresh ginger (from a 1-inch piece)

½ teaspoon red pepper flakes

2 scallions, white and light green parts, thinly sliced

½ cup packed fresh cilantro, leaves and tender stems, finely chopped

1 pound ground chicken, preferably dark meat

2 tablespoons olive oil

1 ripe Hass avocado, sliced, for serving

Toasted brioche buns or other burger buns, for serving

In a small serving bowl, mix together ½ cup of the yogurt, ½ teaspoon of the miso, and the juice of 1 lime and season to taste with salt. Set aside in the fridge until ready to serve.

In a large bowl, mix together the remaining yogurt and miso, the soy sauce, ginger, red pepper flakes, scallions, and cilantro. Add the chicken and gently combine until everything is lightly speckled with green. Divide the mixture evenly into 4 loose balls.

Heat a dry 12-inch cast-iron or other heavy skillet over medium-high heat until hot, about 2 minutes. Pour in the olive oil, tilting the pan until the entire surface is slick with oil. Add the 4 balls, spacing them out, and then use a solid spatula or wooden spoon to smash them into ½-inch-thick patties. Cook, undisturbed, until they easily release from the pan and a brown crust has formed on the bottom, 3 to 4 minutes. Flip and cook until they are no longer pink in the center, about 3 minutes more. Squeeze half a lime over the burgers. Cut the remaining lime half into wedges and use for serving, along with the yogurt, avocado, and buns.

corner sausage patties sandwiches

When I'm nearing the deadline for a book or other big project, it becomes all-consuming, which is something I love, as I really begin to see it all come together. The downside is that the work follows me everywhere, including as I'm about to drift off to sleep and even into my dreams. This recipe came to me in my dreams: I kept hearing "corner sausage patties . . . corner sausage" and picturing it. So I decided to turn these little sausage patties into sandwiches, kind of like the nighttime version of a breakfast sausage sandwich, except with no eggs, just some juicy tomatoes, onions, and melted cheese. Add some pickled jalapeños for an acidic kick and some heat.

Serves 4

1 pint cherry tomatoes or grape tomatoes, halved

1 small red onion, cut into 1-inch-thick wedges

2 tablespoons olive oil, plus more as needed

Salt

¼ to ½ teaspoon red pepper flakes, depending on your heat preference

½ teaspoon dried oregano

2 or 3 garlic cloves, grated or minced

1 pound Italian-style chicken or turkey sausage, removed from its casings

8 slices sourdough or country-style bread

2 to 4 ounces Italian provolone (preferably Auricchio), grated, deli provolone slices, or mozzarella, sliced

¼ cup grated Parmesan

Suggested items for topping: sliced peperoncini, Dijon mustard, fresh basil leaves

Heat the oven to 400°F. Put the tomatoes and onion in the center of a sheet pan. Drizzle with the olive oil and season lightly with salt, the red pepper flakes, oregano, and garlic. Divide the sausage into 4 parts, placing one portion in each corner of the pan, and pat down the sausage to flatten it to about ¼-inch thick and mold it into the corner, almost like brownie corners or pizza squares. On another sheet pan, arrange the slices of bread and drizzle lightly with oil.

Bake in the center of the oven until the tomatoes are juicy and softened and the sausage is cooked through, 20 minutes. Halfway through (aka after 10 minutes, if you set your timer), place the bread on another rack in the oven. Pull it out when the bottom is toasted and the top is browning, 4 to 5 minutes, then flip, lightly coat all the bread with cheese (both sides will have melty bits!), and return it to the oven until melted, 4 to 5 minutes more.

Halve the sausage patties as needed to fit the bread. Sprinkle the tomatoes with the Parmesan and serve family-style right out of the sheet pan with any toppings alongside so everyone can make their own closed or open-faced sandwiches.

big cockle energy
(spicy brothy clams with sausage)

My friend Nicole and I were sitting at the bar for dinner at Here's Looking At You in LA, and we had befriended Curt, a man dining solo next to us. We ordered these cockles, which were so insanely delicious, we had to make sure both Curt and this other person sitting next to us also tried them. Somehow, a few drinks later, we began referring to things as having "Big Cockle Energy." It was one of those nights that remind me how much I love restaurants and meeting new people, plus it inspired this dish. The restaurant's version was served in a rich, ramen-like broth that I'm sure took loads of time to make, but my shortcut version is a quick broth full of flavor makers like miso, garlic, ginger, and scallions, with pork sausage bits that tuck themselves into the little crevices of the cockles (or clams, as those might be easier to find). Share with others or don't—up to you.

Serves 2 generously or 4 with some other dishes

2 tablespoons olive oil

¾ pound hot Italian-style pork sausage, removed from its casings

3 or 4 garlic cloves, grated or minced

1 tablespoon grated or minced fresh ginger (from a 2-inch piece)

1 bunch scallions, light green and white parts only, sliced

1 tablespoon soy sauce

1 (32-ounce) can low-sodium vegetable broth or room-temperature water (4 cups)

1 tablespoon white miso paste

3 pounds cockles or manila or littleneck clams, scrubbed and soaked in cold salted water for 10 minutes if sandy

1 tablespoon chili crisp, plus more for serving

¼ cup fresh cilantro, leaves and tender stems, roughly chopped or torn

Bread, for dipping

Heat the olive oil in a large pot over medium-high heat until shimmering. Add the sausage and cook, breaking it up with a wooden spoon into crumbly pieces and small chunks, until it's browned in spots with no visible pink remaining, 7 to 9 minutes.

Add the garlic, ginger, and two-thirds of the scallions. Cook, stirring occasionally, until fragrant, about 2 minutes. Add the soy sauce and stir until evaporated, about 15 seconds and scrape any brought bits from the bottom of the pot. Pour in the broth and raise the heat to bring the liquid to a gentle boil, then lower the heat to maintain a simmer, add the miso and cockles, cover, and cook until most of the cockles open, 5 to 9 minutes, depending on their size. Discard any that don't open. Stir in the chili crisp, then top with the cilantro and remaining scallions. Serve with bread, the jar of chili crisp, and an empty bowl for the shells.

baked goat cheese meatballs with lime yogurt dip

My first trip to Paris in my late teens was pretty much solely an eating trip (I visited the museums the second go-round), and I became infatuated with salade de chèvre chaud, which is essentially a green salad with a French bistro dressing and thick coins of hot goat cheese, usually sitting on a crunchy slice of bread. I ordered it whenever I could and was pretty much obsessed with it until I finally reached a point where I could no longer bear to look at goat cheese. After a fifteen-year hiatus, I've taken to it again, and have started including it in many of my recipes. Here it's used to make tender, flavorful chicken meatballs served with a lime yogurt dip. The limes make this a juicy sheet pan dish, so it's best served over a grain to soak up the pan juices.

Makes 16 to 18 meatballs

2 tablespoons olive oil, divided, plus more for the pan

2 limes, zested: 1 cut into thin rounds, 1 juiced, seeds poked out

1 cup thick full-fat yogurt, such as Greek yogurt or skyr

¼ teaspoon ground cumin

Salt

4 ounces goat cheese (about ¼ cup)

½ teaspoon dried oregano

½ teaspoon piménton (smoked paprika), plus more for garnish

¼ teaspoon red pepper flakes

¼ cup packed fresh parsley or cilantro, leaves and tender stems, ½ finely chopped, the rest gently torn or chopped, for garnish

1 pound ground chicken or turkey, preferably dark meat

Rice, for serving

Heat the oven to 400°F. Lightly oil a large sheet pan and arrange the lime rounds on it, turning them to coat in the oil.

In a small serving bowl, combine the yogurt, lime juice, cumin, and 1 tablespoon of the olive oil until smooth. Adjust the seasoning as needed with salt. Spoon 1 tablespoon of the yogurt mixture into a large bowl and let the rest sit in the fridge until ready to serve.

Add the goat cheese, lime zest, oregano, paprika, red pepper flakes, 1 teaspoon salt, the chopped herbs, and the remaining tablespoon of olive oil to the large bowl and gently mash together. Add the chicken, combining the ingredients until the mixture is a mild orangey color all over. Lightly oil your hands or wet them with water and shape the mixture into balls, each slightly larger than a golf ball, placing them on the sheet pan around the lime rounds as you work. You will have 16 to 18 balls (more or less is fine, too).

Bake until cooked through, about 15 minutes. Tilt the pan to mix the lime juice and oil together, then spoon the mixture on top of the meatballs. Top the meatballs with the remaining herbs and a light dusting of paprika, and serve with the yogurt dip and rice.

easy, brothy lentil soup

"You're such a weirdo," a friend said as they watched me packing my suitcase after a visit to NYC. It was filled with a collection of spices and two large bags of lentils from Kalustyan's, a legendary Middle Eastern grocer on Lexington Avenue. I do want to note to all travelers that it's likely you'll be stopped at airport security if you're transporting big bags of lentils (and maybe spices, as the powder is concerning), which is what happened to me. None of the security folks seemed amused by my attempts at lentil jokes or my awkward explanations as to why I was transporting them. Anyway, it was all for this recipe! If you'd like to add some sliced carrots or parsnips to this, they would work well. I love eating this in two parts: first, sipping the broth and then straining out the liquid to enjoy the chunky onions, celery, and lentil bites more like a salad, as if they were two separate composed dishes.

Serves 4

1 small yellow onion, thinly sliced

Salt and freshly cracked black pepper

2 tablespoons olive oil

4 celery stalks, thinly sliced

½ teaspoon dried oregano

½ teaspoon ground cumin

½ teaspoon piménton (smoked paprika)

2 tablespoons sherry vinegar or red wine vinegar, plus more if needed

1 cup dried green or brown lentils, rinsed (and soaked for 1 hour or overnight, if you like)

6 cups water (or 2 cups water and 4 cups low-sodium vegetable or chicken broth)

Parmesan rind (optional)

¼ cup packed fresh parsley, leaves and tender stems, gently torn or chopped

¼ cup packed fresh dill leaves, gently torn or chopped (optional)

Heat a dry large Dutch oven over medium-high heat until hot, about 2 minutes. Add the onion to the dry pan, season lightly with salt, and cook, undisturbed, for 2 minutes. Stir, then cook for 2 minutes more. Lower the heat if the onions threaten to burn at any time (a little browning is okay), then raise the heat again when you add the celery. Stir in the olive oil and celery, season with salt, and cook, stirring every minute or so, until soft and silky, about 4 minutes. Add the oregano, cumin, and paprika and cook, stirring, until fragrant, about 30 seconds. Stir in the vinegar and cook until evaporated, about 30 seconds.

Add the lentils, water or broth, and Parmesan rind, if using, season lightly with salt, and bring the liquid to a gentle boil (cover the pot to speed up the process). Adjust the heat to maintain a simmer and cook, uncovered, until the lentils are tender, about 30 minutes. Use a spoon to skim any frothy stuff off the top (I find this meditative). Stir in the herbs, season to taste with salt and a few grinds of pepper, and serve. (If you think it needs more acidity, stir in a splash of vinegar.)

quick note: Use leftover lentils in the lentil salad (page 212) and leftover celery in the salad on page 210.

one-pot spicy lemony sausage + farro soup

"Soup" feels like a generous and perhaps slightly misleading word to use for this one, as it's not brothy and presents more on the slowly-simmered-stew side of things with its depth and heartiness. (We could go into a longer discussion about soup versus stew, but I almost feel like it's the "Is a hot dog a sandwich?" question, which is far too complex to address here.) For this reason, when you reheat it, add a splash of water to loosen it (it also freezes well and has accompanied me on many a tired night when I don't feel like cooking). Skip the beans to make it less hearty or the sausage to make it vegetarian.

Serves 4

2 tablespoons olive oil

1 medium red onion, thinly sliced

Salt

1 pound sausage (pork, chicken, or turkey), removed from its casings

1 small carrot, sliced into rounds

2 teaspoons ground cumin

1 teaspoon ground turmeric

Freshly ground black pepper

1 (28-ounce) can crushed tomatoes

½ cup farro or barley, rinsed

1 small bunch lacinato or curly kale, leaves stemmed and cut into thin strips or roughly torn (about 3 packed cups)

1 (15-ounce) can white beans, such as cannellini or navy, drained and rinsed

1 lemon, halved

½ cup fresh cilantro, leaves and tender stems, roughly chopped

1 jalapeño or Fresno pepper, thinly sliced into rounds

Heat the olive oil in a Dutch oven over medium–high heat until shimmering. Add the onion and a pinch of salt and cook, stirring occasionally, until the onion just starts to soften and lose some of its color, about 3 minutes. Add the sausage and carrot and cook, breaking up the sausage with a wooden spoon into a combination of crumbly bits and small chunks, until no pink remains, 7 to 9 minutes. Stir in the cumin, turmeric, and a few grinds of black pepper and cook until fragrant, about 1 minute more.

Add the tomatoes, 3 cups water, and the farro and bring to a gentle boil (no wild bubbles), then adjust the heat to maintain a gentle simmer. Season generously with salt. Cook, uncovered, until the farro is tender and no longer chewy, about 30 minutes. During the last 10 minutes of cooking, stir in the kale and beans. Squeeze in the lemon juice and stir, then taste and adjust the seasoning as needed. Top with the cilantro and the sliced peppers or serve on the side for everyone to garnish themselves.

roasted chicken thighs with grapes, feta + mint

Early in my graduate school days, a chef friend came over, and as we chatted and sipped some wine, I said I was hungry, and he immediately opened my fridge, pulling out Bulgarian feta and a bag of grapes. In a skillet, he blistered the grapes, finishing them off with a little vinegar, and then seared the feta in the same pan, making it melty and soft, after which we scooped it all up with bread. I still remember the awe of watching his brain work so swiftly as he imagined what he could make with the minimal options in my fridge. This sheet pan version includes chicken thighs seasoned with a little balsamic vinegar and some herbs. The grapes burst and caramelize in the oven, letting out their sweet juices, and some feta chunks are added halfway so they, too, become melty and spreadable.

Serves 4

1 tablespoon olive oil, plus more as needed

2 tablespoons balsamic vinegar, divided

1 tablespoon honey

1 teaspoon dried oregano

2 tablespoons thick full-fat yogurt, such as Greek yogurt or skyr

Salt

2 pounds bone-in, skin-on chicken thighs

1 (6- to 8-ounce) block feta cheese, cut into 1-inch-thick slices

1 pound seedless red grapes, picked from the stems or left in clusters (about 2½ cups)

Freshly cracked black pepper

¼ cup packed fresh mint leaves, gently torn

Crusty bread, for serving

Heat the oven to 400°F. Drizzle the tablespoon of oil on a sheet pan, spreading it out to coat. In a large bowl, combine 1 tablespoon of the vinegar, the honey, oregano, and yogurt, stirring until it forms a thick paste (there won't be a lot). Pat the chicken dry, then season all over with salt and add to the yogurt mixture, coating all over, then place it on the sheet pan, skin-side up. Roast for 20 minutes.

Remove the sheet pan from the oven and nestle the feta between the chicken thighs (it's okay if some break apart or if you need to break them apart to fit). Scatter the grapes around the sheet pan. Drizzle the grapes and feta with the 1 tablespoon olive oil and season the grapes lightly with salt, then use a wooden spoon to nudge and rub the grapes in the oil to coat them. Roast until the feta is melty, the chicken is cooked through, and the grapes deflating and softening in spots, about 20 minutes more. Top with a few grinds of pepper and the mint, and serve with bread.

the mighty vegetable

If you texted me, *How do I cook [blank]?*, this is what I would say

I'm fully that weirdo who talks to all my plants, saying good morning to them, telling them I love them (even kissing them at times), and saying goodbye when I go on a trip—"I'll be back soon and you'll be well taken care of!" I was always limited to indoor plants, filling every room and windowsill with them, until I moved to Miami, where I had a small balcony. Into pots went Sungold tomato, shishito pepper, and jalapeño seeds, lots of basil, rosemary, chives, mint, and so on, until my balcony mostly consisted of pots. I anxiously watered them, waiting for signs of life, talking to them, until finally, delicate little green sprouts popped up. The joy of waking up every morning and stepping outside to see their progress was so much fun, especially when the tomatoes started to show themselves, first as little flowers, then small green balls that ripened into the sweet, sunny gifts that they are.

There's something highly gratifying about growing your own food from seed, nourishing it and watching it develop, waiting and knowing that it all happens at the right time, no matter how impatient or anxious I am. It also showed me how much work and time go into growing a pint of tomatoes—something I can finish on the walk home from the farmers' market. We are so lucky in so many ways to have our food system, but growing your own is also a good reminder of the labor and resources that go into it, much of which we don't see, especially living in large cities.

As trite as it might sound, food is a beautiful way to connect with the earth, ourselves, and one another—and a way to slow down and match the pace of nature (something much easier said than done, for me at least).

This section in particular is meant to help you celebrate vegetables and serve as a reference guide so you can easily make a quick skillet side or a simple sheet pan of vegetables to serve alongside any recipe in this book. You'll find basic cooking instructions, sometimes for both roasting and pan-cooking, sometimes for just one method or the other, if I found it's significantly easier or tastier that way. If you can, cook and eat vegetables in season as that's when they taste the best, preferably from a local source, but if that's not an option for you, then don't worry as I don't want you to feel guilty about that in any way. Sourcing out-of-season ingredients is part of how I'm able to do my job, as I can test asparagus recipes in the dead of winter (even though they're a far cry from the vibrant green stalks found in late spring).

By no means have I covered every vegetable—just the ones I think would be handy as they are already found in other recipes in this book.

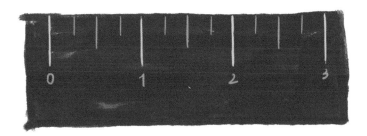

measurement guide for vegetable sizes

This lovely illustration above is based off of the magenta ruler that I bought from a pharmacy on Sixth Avenue many years ago, and which I still keep with me to measure vegetable sizes when I test recipes. (You'll also find it on the spine of the book.)

While having consistently sized vegetables is helpful for even cooking, that's not always the reality, as vegetables grown in the wild tend to be irregularly shaped (I would be wary of anything too perfect looking). Rather than wasting the bits that are too small or not quite right, I like to use them. I actually love when there are varying sizes, as that means you'll also get varying textures: some crispy, crunchy bites along with some soft, creamy ones, if you're roasting butternut squash or potatoes, or heavily charred (bordering on burned) small florets of broccoli with more tender pieces.

Knowing your vegetable size also comes in handy in terms of cooking time. Say you cut them into 1-inch pieces versus ½ inch: The cooking time will be a little bit longer, which is totally fine, but good to know so that you can adjust, especially if you're cooking it alongside a protein like salmon or chicken. Simply take out whichever is done first, the protein or the vegetable, loosely cover it to stay warm, and continue cooking the other.

some fun seasoning ideas

· splash of soy sauce or vinegar
· squeeze of lemon/lime juice

→ scrape up anything on the bottom of the pan

seasonings to use in the pan

(add during the last 30 seconds in the skillet or right out of the oven)

warming + fragrant

mix together:
2 teaspoons grated ginger
   from a 2-inch piece
2 teaspoons ground cumin
¼ teaspoon red-pepper flakes
2 teaspoons white miso paste
1 tablespoon ghee/
   unsalted butter

bright + comforting

mix together:
Zest of 1 lemon, lime, or orange
1 tablespoon ghee or unsalted
   butter
¼ cup fresh flat-leaf parsley,
   rosemary, or thyme, leaves finely
   chopped
1 to 2 garlic cloves, grated or
   minced (optional)

spices for you to play around with

(these can also be used on chicken thighs or a whole chicken)

mediterranean flare + a bit of heat

2 teaspoons dried oregano
2 teaspoons ground cumin
1 teaspoon piménton (smoked
   paprika)
½ teaspoon red-pepper flakes

garlicky + smoky

1 teaspoon smoked paprika
½ teaspoon ground turmeric
½ teaspoon dried oregano
½ teaspoon red-pepper flakes
Freshly cracked black
   pepper
3 cloves garlic, grated or
   minced
1 lime, halved, to squeeze at
   the end

earthy + warming

1 tablespoon ground cumin
1 teaspoon ground turmeric
¼ teaspoon red-pepper flakes
¼ teaspoon freshly cracked black pepper

finishing touches for serving

· flaky sea salt
· freshly cracked black pepper
· red-pepper flakes (always!)
· lemon zest
· soft herbs, gently torn, like basil, mint, parsley, or cilantro
· roasted nuts, like pine or pistachio, or seeds, like pumpkin
· sliced scallions
· grated Parmesan/pecorino, crumbled feta cheese, scoops
  of ricotta, or chunks of mozzarella
· extra-virgin olive oil (your nice one)

vegetable cooking chart

for skillet recipes: 12-inch pan + 2 tablespoons olive oil (or dry, if that's noted) over medium-high heat until shimmering, season with salt

for oven recipes: 400°F on a sheet pan + 2 tablespoons olive oil or more (enough that all pieces are shiny and well coated), season with salt

vegetable	how to prep it	how to cook it
asparagus	**1 bunch:** Snap the stalk at the bottom to remove woody stems as it will naturally break off where needed or cut off chalky-looking bottoms. (Cutting them into bite-size pieces will help them cook a little quicker, too.)	**skillet:** Cook, stirring occasionally, until charred, blistered spots appear and spears are crisp-tender, about 6 minutes, depending on the size. **oven:** Cook, turning halfway, until stalks are crisp-tender but not limp and soggy, 10 to 15 minutes, depending on the thickness.
baby bok choy	**3 or 4 bunches:** Trim the root until the leaves fall apart naturally. Leave whole or cut into bite-size pieces for easier eating. (You can also quarter or halve them lengthwise, without trimming the root, I tend to do that for oven roasting.)	**skillet:** Cook, undisturbed until browned on one side, about 3 minutes. Flip and cook until the other side is brown, leaves crisp and thickest stalk fork tender, 2 to 3 minutes more. **oven:** Cook until thickest part is fork tender and leaves browned, about 12 minutes.
broccoli	**1 small head:** Trim thick stalks and cut the florets into small, bite-size pieces (you'll have about 4 cups).	**skillet:** Cook, undisturbed, for 3 minutes. Turn and cook until fork-tender and browned in spots, 2 to 3 minutes more (larger pieces will take longer). Add a splash of water or soy and cover for 1 to 2 minutes to speed it up. **oven:** Cook for 15 to 20 minutes, until the thickest stalk is fork-tender and the florets are crispy.
broccolini	**1 or 2 bunches:** Trim off the bottom ½ inch and make sure to eat the rest. Thick stalks can be sliced in half lengthwise to cook more quickly and evenly.	**skillet:** Cook, undisturbed, for 2 minutes, then stir. Repeat until charred and crispy, 6 to 8 minutes. **oven:** Cook until the tips are crispy and charred and the stalks are easily pierced with a fork, about 15 minutes.
brussels sprouts	**1 to 2 pounds (or more for the oven):** Trim the root, peel any browned or marked-up outer leaves, then halve. Shred for faster cooking in a skillet.	**skillet:** Cook shredded sprouts, stirring occasionally, until wilted and browned, about 10 minutes. **oven:** Cook until crispy and charred, 25 to 35 minutes, depending on the size of the sprouts.
carrots	**1 bunch:** I don't peel my carrots, but I do scrub them well to remove dirt—if it makes you feel better, go ahead and peel them! Halve thick ones lengthwise so they cook faster.	**skillet:** Cut into coins and cook, undisturbed, for 2 minutes. Stir and repeat, cooking for 2-minute increments, until easily pierced with a fork but not mushy, 6 minutes total. Reduce the heat to medium, add ¼ cup water, cover, and cook until the water has evaporated and the carrots are tender, 4 to 5 minutes more. **oven:** Cook until browned and fork-tender, 25 to 30 minutes. Finish under the broiler for 1 to 3 minutes, depending on the strength of your broiler, for more char and color.

for **skillet recipes:** 12-inch pan + 2 tablespoons olive oil (or dry, if that's noted) over medium-high heat until shimmering, season with salt

for **oven recipes:** 400°F on a sheet pan + 2 tablespoons olive oil or more (enough that all pieces are shiny and well coated), season with salt

vegetable	how to prep it	how to cook it
cauliflower	**1 bunch:** Cut the thick stalks until the florets fall into small, bite-sized pieces.	**oven:** Cook for 40 to 45 minutes, depending on the size of pieces, until caramelized on the bottom.
corn	**2 ears:** Remove the husk and the silky threads, then stand the corn upright in a bowl on its stalk end and use a knife to cut off the kernels, or lay it flat on a cutting board and slice the kernels off.	**broiler:** Broil as much fresh or frozen corn as you can comfortably fit on a sheet pan until the tops become charred, about 7 minutes. .... **skillet:** Spread the corn in an even layer and cook, undisturbed, for 5 minutes. Stir, then cook until the corn starts to crackle and pop and is browned all over, 5 to 6 minutes more, stirring halfway.
kale (also chard + collard greens)	**1 bunch:** Form a hook with your index and middle fingers, turn the kale or collard so the stalk is facing up and the leaf down, and scrape your fingers on either side of the stalk to remove the leaf. Tear or cut the leaves into ribbons. For chard, you can eat the stalk; it needs to be cooked for a couple of minutes more than the leaves. Trim the end of the stalk, slice into ½-inch pieces or so, and cook before the leaves.	**skillet:** Cook, stirring every couple of minutes, until the leaves have softened and shrunk down slightly and colored in spots, 5 to 6 minutes total. .... **oven:** Cook until crunchy and charred in spots, 15 to 20 minutes.
mushrooms	**1 to 2 pounds:** Most mushroom stems are edible, other than shiitakes, which have to be removed, so you can just trim the woody end bits. Use a damp paper towel to rub off any visible dirt on the mushrooms. If they are very, very dirty, you can wash them, but you will have to cook them even longer in a dry skillet to get rid of the excess water. Slice them thinly, quarter them, or leave small ones whole.	**skillet:** Heat a dry skillet over medium-high heat until very hot, about 2 minutes. Add the mushrooms in an even layer and cook, without moving them, for 2 minutes. Season lightly with salt and then spread them out over the pan and cook, undisturbed, for 2 minutes more. Repeat until the mushrooms are starting to brown and you've seen wet droplets on their surface evaporate, 4 to 8 minutes more. Stir in 1 to 2 tablespoons olive oil or a mixture of oil and ghee, and cook until browned, 2 to 3 minutes more.
baby potatoes	**1½ to 2 pounds:** I don't peel them, but I do scrub them clean of dirt. The flesh will oxidize and turn brown if you leave it exposed to air for too long, so cut them right before using. Halve or quarter larger ones.	**oven:** Cook until crispy on the outside and easily pierced with a fork, 40 to 55 minutes, depending on the size, stirring halfway.

for **skillet recipes:** 12-inch pan + 2 tablespoons olive oil (or dry, if that's noted) over medium-high heat until shimmering, season with salt

for **oven recipes:** 400°F on a sheet pan + 2 tablespoons olive oil or more (enough that all pieces are shiny and well coated), season with salt

vegetable	how to prep it	how to cook it
radishes	**1 pound:** Scrub the outsides well to remove dirt and reserve the greens for cooking. Trim the little white beards and halve them or quarter large ones.	**skillet radish greens:** Cook until wilted and tender, 6 to 8 minutes. **oven:** Cook for 20 minutes, until easily pierced with a fork and tender.
squash	**1 to 2 squash:** Halve and scoop out the seeds for all squash. Delicata skin can be eaten, while the others need to be peeled, which is easier after cooking.	**oven, for halved butternut, acorn, and honeynut squash:** Cook cut-side down until the flesh is tender and easily pierced with a fork and the skin is bubbling and browned, 35 to 60 minutes, depending on the size of the squash. **oven, 1-inch cubes:** Cook until easily pierced with a fork, 25 to 40 minutes. **oven, for 1 delicata squash:** Cut into half-moon pieces and cook until the bottom is caramelized and the flesh starts to look translucent in parts and is easily pierced with a fork, 25 to 30 minutes.
sweet potato	**1 medium potato:** Scrub clean, leaving the skin on unless it bothers you, and trim the ends if cutting into pieces.	**oven, wrapped in foil:** Prick the potato in a few places on the top with the tines of a fork or the tip of a sharp knife, then wrap loosely in foil and bake until tender and creamy, about 30 minutes for small to medium ones or up to 1 hour for larger ones. Let cool slightly, then pry open and leave to cool until you can easily handle it. **oven, wedges:** Quarter 1 medium sweet potato lengthwise, then cut each quarter into 3 or 4 wedges, about ½-inch thick. Cook until crispy at the edges and fork-tender, 25 to 30 minutes. **oven, cubed:** Cut in half through the equator, then cut each piece in half lengthwise and then into ½-inch cubes. Cook until fork-tender, about 25 minutes.
zucchini + summer squashes	**1 or 2 medium ones:** Trim the ends, no need to peel as the skin is delicate. Halve them, and scoop out the sliver of seeds inside, as they can make a dish too watery.	**skillet, cut into cubes or half moons:** Cook, stirring occasionally, until browned all over and tender, 10 to 12 minutes. **broiler, cut into spears:** Cook until the tops start to char and darken, about 5 minutes, depending on your broiler. Turn over and cook until charred on the other side and can easily be pierced with a fork, 3 to 4 minutes more. **oven, cut into spears:** Cook until browned on the bottom and tender, 15 to 20 minutes.

Welcome to the food + wine pairing chart!

Much like you can navigate a bar menu by picking the category of drink you want—sweet, citrusy, refreshing, spirit-forward—you can now do that with the recipes in this book! Allegra Angelo, sommelier and cofounder of Vinya Wine & Market in Miami, Florida, has written the descriptions and pairings in the chart, and you can easily take these tips to your local wine shop or search for her recommendations online. (Thank you, Allegra!) Once you pick the dish you want to make, use the recipe title to guide you to the dominant ingredient of the dish and match it up with the headings in the chart (sometimes there will be more than one dominant ingredient, so pick your favorite or look at Allegra's tip for navigating spreads). Or, if you have a bottle of sparkling rosé or a chilled red, let that lead you to a good recipe to make.

We hope you enjoy these pairings—safe and happy drinking!

wine pairing chart (!!)

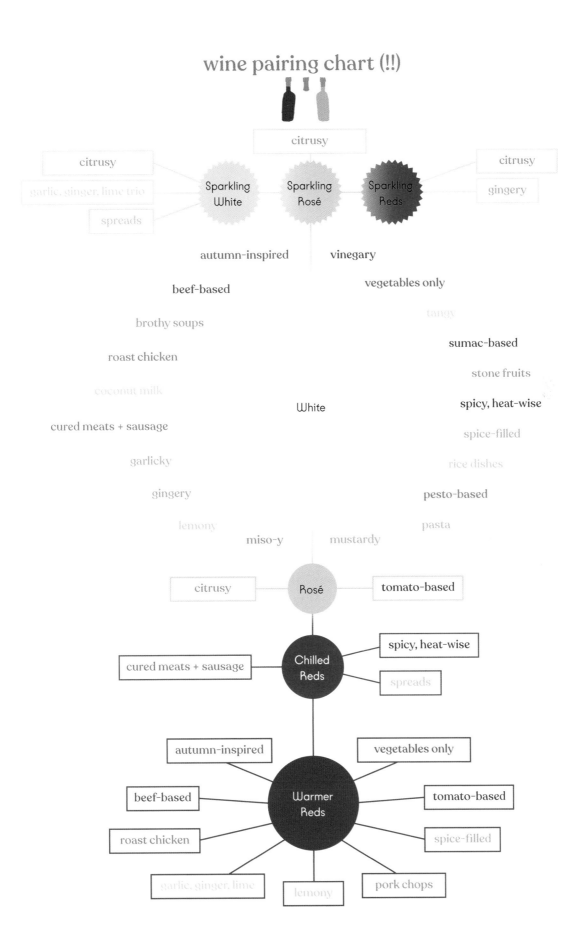

citrusy

citrusy   **Sparkling White**   **Sparkling Rosé**   **Sparkling Reds**   citrusy

garlic, ginger, lime trio   gingery

spreads

autumn-inspired   vinegary

beef-based   vegetables only

brothy soups   tangy

sumac-based

roast chicken   stone fruits

coconut milk   spicy, heat-wise

White   spice-filled

cured meats + sausage   rice dishes

garlicky

gingery   pesto-based

lemony   pasta

miso-y   mustardy

citrusy   **Rosé**   tomato-based

spicy, heat-wise

cured meats + sausage   **Chilled Reds**

spreads

autumn-inspired   vegetables only

beef-based   **Warmer Reds**   tomato-based

roast chicken   spice-filled

garlic, ginger, lime   lemony   pork chops

autumn-inspired (apples, mushrooms, and so on)	Chenin blanc and syrah were meant for autumn. Chenin blanc smells like apples and crisp leaves, and syrah feels like a cozy sweater. Look for a bigger style of chenin blanc from places like Savennières or California's Dry Creek Valley. For syrah, explore lean styles from places like the Côte-Rôtie or Australia's Yarra Valley.	chenin blanc syrah
beef-based (meat sauce or kebabs)	Dare to break the rules and stray from a red wine and pairing in lieu of a richer white wine: try a dry gewürztraminer from Alsace or Northern Italy. Or, play it safe with a merlot from Bordeaux or a syrah from Walla Walla in Washington State.	gewürztraminer merlot, syrah
brothy soups (+ dishes, too)	Broaden the flavors of brothy dishes by pairing with opulent, white Rhône varietals. The grapes to know are: marsanne, viognier, roussanne, and white grenache. Explore places like the Southern Rhône, Paso Robles, or South Africa's Swartland region.	marsanne, viognier, roussanne, white grenache
citrusy (orange family)	Orange colored citrus is typically associated with white wines, but sparkling wines, rosé, and red wines cover a rainbow of citrus, too. Look for a blanc des blancs from Champagne, a deeply colored cerasuolo from Abruzzo, or a frappato from Sicily.	blanc des blancs (Champagne) cerasuolo frappato
coconut milk	Beer is ideal because its bitterness cuts the coconut milk's richness. Wine is trickier, but not impossible. Opt for riper, aged expressions of bitter white grapes. Start with these three: Spain's albariño, Austria's grüner veltliner, and Italy's verdicchio.	albariño, grüner veltliner, verdicchio
cured meats sausage + (salami + jamón)	Dishes speckled with these meats crave acidity in wines. The best pairings are off-dry whites and chillable, wafer-thin reds. Look for an expression of Vouvray (chenin blanc) referred to as sec tendre (tender dry). In reds, explore the native Piedmont grapes like barbera, dolcetto, freisa, and grignolino.	Vouvray (chenin blanc) barbera, dolcetto, freisa, grignolino
garlicky	Garlic is funky, in a good way. It plays well with white grapes that naturally have a lower acidity. Ask your local wine merchant for a marsanne from the Northern Rhône of France, a not-so oaky viognier from California, or a bold friulano from Italy.	marsanne, viognier, friulano
garlic, ginger, lime trio	Bubbles and juicy reds with low tannins enhance these flavors. For bubbles, try Spain's new organic Cava appellation called "Corpinnat." For reds, look for a tutti-frutti grolleau from France or the rare, white spice pelaverga from Italy's Piedmont region.	Corpinnat tutti-frutti grolleau, pelaverga
gingery	Ginger has a pungent spice that hits you on the back end of the palate—pair it with aromatic whites and dark red sparkling wines. Try a peachy Riesling from Germany's Rheingau, a nutty-honey chenin blanc from France's Vouvray, or a dry style of lambrusco from Italy's Emilia-Romagna.	Riesling, chenin blanc lambrusco
lemony	Lemon has a juicy acidity that syncs with both white and red grapes that have an underbelly of sweet citrus. For whites, try a sauvignon blanc from Napa Valley or a pecorino from Abruzzo. For reds, try gaglioppo from Calabria or jaen from Portugal.	sauvignon blanc, pecorino gaglioppo, jaen
miso-y	Miso loves textural white wines that match its salt-lick core personality. Choose "salty" grapes, typically aged in steel or used oak barrels, like albariño from Galicia, vermentino from Sardinia, or chardonnay from Chablis.	albariño, vermentino, chardonnay
mustardy	Mustard needs a wine that can hold up to its big personality. Try something more funky, like a skin contact white from the Mediterranean (think Corsica or Sardinia), a volcanic soil listán blanco from the Canary Islands, or a floral malagousia from Greece.	listán blanco, malagousia
pasta (simple, lemony, cheesy, but no tomatoes!)	Pasta loves wine. For lighter styles, seasoned with lemon and cheese, choose white grapes that express a wavy texture on the palate. Roam the globe with an encruzado from Portugal, a carricante from Sicily, or pinot blanc from Oregon. And remember, it doesn't have to be Italian!	encruzado, carricante, pinot blanc
pesto-based	Fuller-bodied Italian white grapes make magic with pesto. Look for the Riesling-like timorasso from Piedmont and the ancient nosiola grape from the Dolomites. In Veneto, explore a higher-end soave made from the garganega grape, and on the Adriatic coast, search for an aged verdicchio or pecorino.	timorasso, nosiola, garganega, aged verdicchio, aged pecorino

pork chops	Whether tangy, tart, or spicy, pork enjoys a glass of pinot noir. Beyond France, Oregon, and California, look for moderate alcohol (12.5% to 13.5%) and from the following places: Central Otago in New Zealand, Argentina's Mendoza, and Chile's San Antonio Valley.	●	pinot noir
rice (with a little something else)	Splurge on a mineral-thick Burgundian chardonnay from iconic places like Meursault or Chassagne-Montrachet. If you're on a budget, then find extraordinary value in appellations of Pernand-Vergelesses and Savigny-lès-Beaune. For rice dishes with bold spices, follow the spice-filled suggestions.		chardonnay
roast chicken (simply seasoned dishes)	You can't ignore the obvious French three with a perfect roast chicken: pinot noir, gamay, and syrah. Feeling more adventurous? Try a bold and smoky castelão from Portugal or the red-fruited carignan from places like France, Lebanon, or Sierra Nevada foothills of California.	●	pinot noir, gamay, syrah, castelão, carignan
roast chicken (lots of spices + herbs)	Herbs and spices with chicken elevate the palate toward bolder pairings. For whites, try a full-bodied rebula from Slovenia, also known as ribolla gialla in Italy. For reds, look for savory Southern Rhône grapes: grenache, syrah, and mourvèdre. You can find these grapes in the underrated wine regions of Beaumes-de-Venise, Gigondas, and Vacqueyras.	●	rebula .... grenache, syrah, mourvèdre
spicy, heat-wise	Spicy is one of the most fun wine pairings. Softly sweet whites soothe the palate, as well as light and silky reds. Try a textural pinot gris from Alsace, a classic Riesling Spätlese from Germany, or a chilled light red, like trousseau!	●	pinot gris, Riesling Spätlese .... trousseau
spice-filled (lots of turmeric, cumin, paprika…)	All colors of wine can express similar bold spice notes after some time in the bottle. For a sensory stimulating "matchy-matchy" pairing try an old-school white rioja from Spain, a golden sémillon from Australia, or a big carménère from Chile. Look for vintages from 2005 to 2015.	●	rioja, golden sémillon .... carménère
spreads (+ snacking plates)	Light fizzy wines and chilled reds are a great way to cleanse the palate after you dip. For fizzy, search-out the term "pét-nat," short for "pétillant naturel." For chilled reds, look for the jovial grapes: gamay, mencía, pineau d'aunis, and trousseau.	○ ●	pét-nat .... gamay, mencía, pineau d'aunis, and trousseau
stone fruits	Search for wines that are lush and tropical. Warmer-climate, but balanced, chardonnays, rieslings, and sauvignon blancs will do the trick, just make sure they're not too oaky. Search out producers from the Santa Cruz Mountains, Austria's Wachau, and the Adelaide Hills of Australia.		chardonnay, riesling, sauvignon blanc
sumac-based	Sumac works with big whites that match its citrus flavor. A floral muscat from Alsace is a unique pairing that works by contrast. While a sauvignon blanc-sémillon blend from Bordeaux is a more classic choice and works by complement.		muscat, sauvignon blanc-sémillon
tangy (feta or yogurt)	Tangy yogurt or feta dishes crave white wines that spend extended time on their lees (spent cells that precipitate to the bottom after fermentation), which make them textural and almost "cheesy." Try a premier cru chablis, a godello from Spain, or grüner veltliner from Austria.		chablis, godello, grüner veltliner
tomato-based (pasta + other dishes)	A versatile and friendly ingredient! For lighter dishes think pink: a classic Provence style or a grenache-based rosé from Spain. For bolder tomato-based dishes, choose earthy, medium-bodied reds like a tempranillo from rioja, a sangiovese from Chianti Classico, or an old-vine cinsault from Lebanon.	○ ●	provence style or grenache-based-rosé .... tempranillo, sangiovese, cinsault
vegetables only	Let the colorful ingredients be the star of the show and pair by contrast. Choose wines that are more neutral on the nose and less over-the-top on the palate, like a pinot bianco from Alto Adige, an aligoté from Burgundy, or a pinot noir from Santa Rita Hills.	●	pinot bianco, aligoté pinot noir
vinegary (salad dressings or vinegary side dishes)	Acid likes acid. Search for grapes that grow in very cold climates and leave your taste buds feeling fresh and clean–like a bone-dry Riesling from Germany's Saar region, a tart chenin blanc from France's saumur, or a lightly oaked chardonnay from the extremes of Patagonia.		Riesling, chenin blanc, chardonnay

at the dinner table

3

i feel great. i'm sleeping well and am excited to cook!

for times when you have more energy and are feeling enthusiastic (yay!)

Whenever I'm seated at a bar counter or communal table in a restaurant, I always think, *This can go one of two ways.* Either my new dining buddies are really interesting, cool people and we have some fun conversations, maybe even share some food—it's happened, multiple times. Or the people are cold and not into food and, worst of all, complain about everything—this also, unfortunately, happens.

Some of my more interesting travel and dining experiences have been at these shared, close-quartered spaces, in tiny restaurants with a minuscule amount of room between tables, or alone at the bar.

One time, in Barcelona, I was at Bar Bodega Quimet, the more chilled-out sister to Quimet & Quimet, and an older retired couple from Seattle were seated very close to me. With their kids grown up and out of the house, they had decided to spend three months of every year living in a new place—how cool is that? They had picked the Gràcia neighborhood of Barcelona (my favorite part of the city, too) for that year. I sipped vermut while we talked about the menu, travel, Barcelona, and their favorite local spots. They even taught me some helpful Catalan words for ordering. I left inspired to follow their lead when I retire. Another joyful time, my friends Joni, Anna, and I broke out in song with the women sitting next to us at the communal table at Via Carota in New York City when we learned they were celebrating their mom's birthday.

There's something intimate about sharing a meal with people, whether you know them or not, whether you're actually sharing plates or just eating side by side, that forges a bond and breaks down the barriers we typically surround ourselves with, especially if they also have an appreciation and love for food and dining. And while I love eating out at restaurants for both the food and the experience, there's something equally special about sharing a meal with others at home, whether that's your own family or friends who are like family.

This section is for both when you're feeding a larger crowd and when you have a bit more energy and time to spend in the kitchen (nothing will take too long, I promise!). I would even argue that some of the recipes are easy enough for a weeknight dinner. Many are intentionally designed to cook in the oven without much interference, so you can use that time to make stovetop dishes and salads to bulk up the meal when having people over or make these on a weeknight, so you can put your feet up and relax while the oven does the work for you. Take, for example, the Crispy Lemony-Yogurt Chicken for a Crowd, where you make a ton of chicken and use that cooking time to make some salads and/or sides found at the end of this chapter (page 199), to go with it, and serve everything family-style. That's what I do, though I might add the mushroomy farro dish or a pasta too, if it's a larger crew. There are also easy, foolproof fish dishes that follow this same oven-cooking format.

Some of these recipes are for when you want to spend a little bit of time lingering in the kitchen, enjoying that time as your focus, rather than simply getting dinner on the table (both are valid and real). Take the Baked Tomato Mac n' Cheese (page 171), a pot of pure comfort with its tomato base. It takes a tiny bit more time, and something I would never ask you to make on a Monday night. But on a chilly Sunday with some friends coming over in cozy clothes? Yes, definitely then.

garlicky shrimp with angel hair pasta

Way back in the day, there was a restaurant called Marco Solo in the now-defunct Atrium mall in Chestnut Hill, Massachusetts, where I grew up. Their shrimp pasta was one of those dishes that made a chatty, squirmy kid like me go silent, twirling the noodles on my fork by gently resting it in my spoon, then closing my eyes as I led it to my mouth (in hindsight, I don't know why I closed my eyes). Slices of garlic, plump, seared shrimp with burst tomatoes, and thin angel hair pasta–I loved it so. I was very, very sad when the restaurant closed, and I've been re-creating this pasta ever since, which comes together very quickly considering how satisfying it is.

Serves 4

2 tablespoons tomato paste

6 garlic cloves: 3 grated or minced, 3 thinly sliced

½ teaspoon ground oregano

½ teaspoon piménton (smoked paprika)

¼ teaspoon red pepper flakes, plus more as desired

1 pound peeled and deveined shrimp patted dry, tails on or off

Salt

¾ pound angel hair pasta or other long, thin noodles (use the rest of the box in the kale + ginger soup on page 92!)

2 tablespoons olive oil

2 anchovies, preferably packed in oil

2 pints cherry tomatoes or grape tomatoes

½ cup white wine, preferably what you're drinking

1 tablespoon unsalted butter or ghee

Extra-virgin olive oil

2 tablespoons packed fresh parsley, leaves and tender stems, gently torn

In a large bowl, combine the tomato paste, grated garlic, oregano, paprika, and red pepper flakes. Pat the shrimp dry, then coat in the spice mixture (it won't perfectly stick to the shrimp, which is fine!).

Bring a large pot of well-salted water to a boil. Add the angel hair and cook until just shy of al dente, 2 to 3 minutes less than the package instructions. Drain.

Meanwhile, heat the olive oil and anchovies in a 12-inch skillet over medium-high heat, letting the anchovies melt into the oil, until the oil is shimmering, about 1 minute. Add the tomatoes, season lightly with salt, and cook until the skins just start to blister, about 4 minutes (the oil will likely splatter, and I'm sorry about that!). Carefully give them a poke with a sharp knife if they aren't breaking down.

Add the shrimp, scraping anything remaining in the bowl into the pan, then add the sliced garlic and a pinch of red pepper flakes, if desired, and cook until the shrimp are pink on the bottom and the tomatoes look punched in, about 2 minutes. Flip the shrimp, add the wine and butter, and let it bubble away for 1 minute more. Stir in the pasta and toss to combine with the tomatoes and shrimp, then cook until warmed through, about 2 minutes more. Drizzle with extra-virgin olive oil and sprinkle with parsley and more red pepper flakes, if desired.

baked chicken meatballs with orange-honey yogurt dip

While in Spain, I found a yogurt that I was obsessed with, one that tasted so delicious that there had to be something added to it. I lived in a blissful state of denial, as I couldn't read the label, until I finally admitted to myself the truth I had known all along: there was honey in it. This recipe was inspired by that sweet honey yogurt, which both goes into the meatballs and serves as a dipping sauce. These meatballs are full of bright, citrusy, and earthy flavors. They'd pair well with some orzo lightly dressed with lemon and olive oil and a little drizzle of the yogurt for a more substantial meal. While the citrus is cut into wedges for easy squeezing at the end, you could cut it into thin rounds instead.

Makes 16 to 18 meatballs

3 tablespoons olive oil, divided, plus more as needed

1 cup thick full-fat yogurt, such as Greek yogurt or skyr, or labneh

1 seedless orange, such as Cara Cara or navel, halved and ½ cut into ½-inch-thick wedges

2 teaspoons honey

Salt

¼ teaspoon red pepper flakes

2 teaspoons packed grated or minced fresh ginger (from a 2-inch piece)

2 garlic cloves, grated

2 scallions, white and light green parts, thinly sliced

1 teaspoon dried oregano

1 teaspoon ground cumin

3 tablespoons panko bread crumbs or old-fashioned rolled oats

2 tablespoons packed fresh basil, finely chopped, plus gently torn leaves for garnish

1 pound ground chicken, preferably dark meat

Heat the oven to 400°F. Drizzle a sheet pan with 2 tablespoons olive oil, using your hands or a brush to evenly coat the surface.

In a small serving bowl, combine the yogurt, 2 tablespoons of orange juice from the halved orange, and the honey. Scoop ¼ cup of the yogurt mixture into a large bowl for the meatballs. Season the remaining yogurt mixture with salt to taste, then place in the fridge until ready to eat.

Add the red pepper flakes, ginger, garlic, scallions, oregano, cumin, bread crumbs, chopped basil, and 1 teaspoon salt to the large bowl and mix to combine. Add the chicken and gently combine until the mixture is lightly speckled with green. Lightly oil or wet your palms so the mixture won't stick and form it into balls, each slightly larger than a golf ball, rolling them with a feathery touch and placing them on the prepared sheet pan as you work. You should have 16 to 18 meatballs. If any balls are on the larger side (it happens), place them around the pan edges, as it's hotter there. Rub the orange wedges with 1 tablespoon olive oil and scatter them around the chicken, cut-side down.

Cook, rotating the pan halfway through, until no longer pink in the middle, about 15 minutes. Squeeze some of the orange wedges over the meatballs, scatter some basil leaves on top, and serve with the yogurt. Or spread the yogurt over the bottom of a large plate or platter and place the meatballs on top so people can easily scoop and dip. (Pour any pan juices on top, too.)

baked white fish with citrusy olive + herb topping

Citrus slices are the colorful cushion for the fish, preventing it from sticking to the pan while also infusing it with a bit of flavor. If you're preparing this ahead for a crowd, then make the citrusy topping in the first step, cover and reserve in the fridge and then proceed with step two when you're ready to cook the meal. Serve with leftover celery salad (page 210) or zucchini salad (page 208).

Serves 4

¼ teaspoon red pepper flakes

½ teaspoon ground cumin

Salt

2 limes: 1 zested and juiced (about 2 tablespoons juice), 1 thinly sliced

2 navel oranges: 1 juiced (about ¼ cup juice), 1 thinly sliced

2 tablespoons olive oil, plus more as needed

1 small shallot, cut into rings

1 cup green olives, such as Castelvetrano, smashed, pitted, and roughly chopped (see page 67)

1½ pounds white-fleshed fish, such as cod or halibut, cut into 4- to 6-ounce fillets, 1 to 1½ inches thick

½ teaspoon piménton (smoked paprika)

½ cup packed fresh cilantro, leaves and tender stems, gently torn or chopped

¼ cup packed fresh mint, leaves, gently torn or chopped (optional)

Freshly cracked black pepper

In a medium bowl, whisk together the red pepper flakes, cumin, a little salt, the lime zest, lime juice, and orange juice. Whisk in 1 tablespoon of the olive oil. Stir in the shallot, then set aside.

Heat the oven to 400°F. Heat the remaining olive oil in a medium skillet over medium-high heat until shimmering. Add the olives and cook, stirring occasionally, until blistered in spots, about 4 minutes. Remove from the heat and let cool slightly, then add to the bowl with the citrus mixture.

On a sheet pan, arrange the orange and lime slices. Lay the fish fillets on top of them, season all over with salt, then drizzle with oil. Sprinkle the paprika on the tops and sides until the fish is mostly a reddish color, gently rubbing it in with your hands (wear gloves if you like). Bake until the fish is flaky and just barely cooked through, about 10 minutes for 1-inch-thick fillets, 12 to 15 minutes for 1½-inch-thick fillets.

Right before serving, add the herbs to the citrusy mix and toss to combine. Top the fish fillets with a little bit of the herb mixture and a few grinds of black pepper, and serve the remaining herb mix on the side.

quick thought: Pitting the olives is a time-intensive process, but one that can be meditative, especially if you enjoy sneaking bites and nibbling leftover meat from the pits. If that's not your thing, buy pitted olives.

creamy charred corn + jalapeño pasta
(with miso and coconut milk)

Creamy, crunchy, full of flavor, and topped with limey scallions—I love this pasta so much. I first made it in Maine, with local corn, on a rainy, hot, and humid day, and then again in Miami, with frozen corn, on a hot, humid day. It is great because you can make it year-round with frozen corn, and it feels light enough to eat on a hot day. You can also leave out the pasta if you'd rather serve it with bread to soak up the rich, coconutty sauce, like a loose stew of sorts.

Serves 4

Salt

1 bunch scallions, light green and white parts only, thinly sliced

1 red Fresno pepper or jalapeño, sliced into rounds

2 limes, halved

½ cup packed fresh cilantro, leaves and tender stems, gently torn or chopped

1 pound short curly dried pasta, such as cavatappi or fusilli

2 tablespoons olive oil, plus more as needed

4 ears of corn, kernels removed, or 1 (1-pound) bag frozen sweet corn kernels (about 3 cups)

1 teaspoon ground cumin

1 teaspoon dried oregano

½ teaspoon red pepper flakes

1 tablespoon white miso paste

1 (13.5-ounce) can full-fat coconut milk

½ cup grated Parmesan

Bring a large pot of well-salted water to a boil. Meanwhile, put the scallions in a small bowl with the Fresno rounds. Squeeze 1 lime into it and season lightly with salt, stirring to coat, then toss with the cilantro. Set aside.

Add the pasta to the boiling water and cook until just shy of al dente, 2 or 3 minutes less than the package instructions. Drain and leave in the the colander in the sink. If the corn isn't ready yet, drizzle with olive oil and toss so it doesn't stick.

Once the pasta is in the pot, heat the olive oil in a 12-inch skillet or Dutch oven over medium-high heat until shimmering. Add the corn, season lightly with salt, and spread out in an even layer. Cook, without stirring, until some of the kernels are browned on the bottom and the corn is crackling and popping, about 4 minutes. Cook, stirring occasionally, until half the corn has some color on it, about 5 minutes more. Mix in the cumin, oregano, and red pepper flakes and cook until fragrant, about 30 seconds. Then add the miso and coconut milk, stirring to mix the solids and liquids until smooth, and adjust the heat to maintain a simmer (avoid a boil). Cook until slightly thickened and reduced, about 4 minutes.

Pour in the pasta and Parmesan, reduce the heat to low, and stir until the pasta is coated with the sauce and combined, about 1 minute more. Remove from the heat and squeeze in a lime half, then cut the remaining lime half into wedges. Taste and season as needed with more lime or salt, then top the pasta with some of the limey scallion mixture and serve the rest alongside with the lime wedges.

honey-orange chicken with feta, cumin + ginger

During my extended stay in Menorca, as I was bouncing from home to home, I lucked out with a dreamy artist's escape that was also a short walk to a local swimming hole and featured a writing desk overlooking the water. It was the home of Nuria Roman, a wonderful artist who lives in the equally stunning studio and home a yard away from the house. I invited her over for a late lunch outdoors, with the dappled sunlight peppering the wooden table set with this sticky-sweet and golden chicken, a light salad, some fresh bread, and a chilled white wine. I loved her kitchen—it was full of life and whimsy, with sky-blue walls dotted with yellow flowers she painted herself, and a blue stovetop. Simply a lovely place to cook.

Serves 4

1 tablespoon honey

1 tablespoon ground cumin

2 teaspoons grated or minced fresh ginger (from a 2-inch piece)

1 teaspoon red pepper flakes

1 small orange: ½ thinly sliced and seeded, ½ juiced (about 1 tablespoon)

2 tablespoons olive oil, divided

2½ pounds bone-in, skin-on chicken parts, such as thighs or drumsticks

Salt

½ cup crumbled feta

¼ cup packed fresh basil or mint leaves, gently torn or chopped

In a large bowl, mix the honey, cumin, ginger, red pepper flakes, orange juice, and 1 tablespoon of the olive oil until mostly smooth (the honey will be a little clumpy). Pat the chicken dry, then season all over with salt. Add to the honey mixture and toss to coat well, sneaking some under the skin, if you like. Let sit at room temperature for 15 to 30 minutes or cover and marinate in the fridge overnight.

Heat the oven to 400°F. Drizzle the remaining 1 tablespoon oil over a sheet pan, then add the orange slices and turn them over to coat in the oil and rub around the pan. Place the chicken skin-side up on the pan. Cook until the juices run clear when poked with a knife and the skin is crispy, about 40 minutes. Scatter the feta and basil on top and serve.

summery pasta with vegetables + goat cheese

I know you probably don't want to turn the oven on during the summer, which I fully get, but as someone yet to be blessed in life with their own grill, given my city choices, sometimes you just have to. You can definitely grill these vegetables instead if you're one of the lucky ones, as it's more about cooking them to your liking and then adding them to the cooked pasta. I became obsessed with the combination of cumin, ricotta, zucchini, and mint back in my *Food & Wine* magazine days; they published a chef's recipe with these ingredients, and it felt like a revelation. My summer squash recipes have been inspired ever since, so this recipe draws on that flavor profile but uses goat cheese as the creamy substitute for the ricotta.

Serves 4 to 6

1 large or 2 small zucchini or summer squash, halved lengthwise, seeded, and cut into ½-inch-thick half-moons

1 pint grape tomatoes or cherry tomatoes

2 ears of corn, kernels removed (about 2 cups)

4 or 5 garlic cloves, peeled and smashed

½ teaspoon ground cumin

¼ teaspoon red pepper flakes (or less, depending on your heat preference)

Salt

3 tablespoons olive oil

1 pound short tubular pasta, such as ziti, fusilli, or cavatappi

4 ounces goat cheese

¼ cup grated Parmesan

½ cup packed fresh mint or basil leaves, finely chopped

Zest and juice of 1 lemon

Heat the oven to 400°F. On a sheet pan, combine the squash, tomatoes, corn, garlic, cumin, and red pepper flakes and season with salt. Add the olive oil and toss to combine. Spread the ingredients evenly over the pan and roast until the vegetables are browned and most of the tomatoes have burst and look like deflated punching bags, 30 to 35 minutes.

After 20 minutes, bring a large pot of well-salted water to a boil. Add the pasta, lowering the heat so the bubbles aren't scary and angry looking, and cook until the pasta is just shy of al dente, about 2 minutes less than the package instructions. Reserve 1 cup of the pasta water, then drain. Leave in the sink if the vegetables aren't quite done yet.

Return the pasta to the pot without wiping it out and set it over low heat. Scrape in everything on the sheet pan, then stir in ½ cup of the reserved pasta water, the goat cheese, Parmesan, and half the mint until smooth and creamy. Add a splash more pasta water as needed if it looks dry. Stir in the lemon zest and half the lemon juice. Taste, season with salt and more lemon juice as needed, then top with the remaining mint and serve.

gingery chicken meatballs with coconut rice

The few times I made this, I found myself standing over the sheet pan, popping piping-hot meatballs into my mouth (because, you know, I *had* to make sure they were seasoned properly), then spooning the equally hot rice into my mouth, burning myself in the process, forgetting momentarily that I should also take a photo. While the ingredient list might look annoying, it's more so that you it prep all at once and divide, rather than doing it multiple times. Serve with citrusy kale + Brussels salad (page 216) or lime-ginger radishes (page 220).

Makes 16 to 18 meatballs

2 tablespoons olive oil, divided, plus more for the meatballs

3 garlic cloves, grated or minced

1 tablespoon grated fresh ginger (from a 3-inch piece), divided

1 bunch scallions, light green and white parts separated and thinly sliced

2 tablespoons mayonnaise, preferably Kewpie

2 tablespoons soy sauce, divided

Salt

½ teaspoon red pepper flakes

1 cup packed fresh cilantro, leaves and tender stems (about 1 bunch), finely chopped

2 tablespoons panko bread crumbs

1 pound ground chicken, preferably dark meat

1 lime, halved

1 (13.5-ounce) can full-fat coconut milk

2 cups jasmine rice

1 Fresno pepper or jalapeño, thinly sliced into rounds

Heat the oven to 400°F. Drizzle 1 tablespoon of the olive oil over a sheet pan, tilting it or using your hands to coat the surface.

In a large bowl, combine the garlic, half the ginger, the light green scallions, the mayonnaise, 1 tablespoon of the soy sauce, ½ teaspoon salt, and the red pepper flakes. Add most of the chopped cilantro (reserve some for garnish) to the bowl and mix until paste-like. Add the panko and ground chicken, lightly mixing until it looks more or less speckled with green spots. Wet your hands with water or oil, then shape the mixture into balls, each slightly larger than a golf ball, placing them on the prepared sheet pan as you go. Bake until barely cooked through, 14 minutes. Squeeze ½ lime over the meatballs and set aside until the rice is ready.

Meanwhile, heat the remaining 1 tablespoon oil in a Dutch oven or braising dish with a tight-fitting lid over medium-high heat until shimmering. Add the scallion whites and cook, stirring, until they start to brown, about 1 minute, then add the remaining ginger and cook until fragrant, about 30 seconds more. Pour in the coconut milk, 2 cups water, the remaining soy sauce, and ½ teaspoon salt, then add the rice, stirring to combine and dissolve any coconut chunks. Bring the mixture to a simmer, cover, and cook, stirring occasionally to make sure nothing is sticking to the bottom, until the rice is tender and has absorbed most of the liquid, about 20 minutes total.

Squeeze in the juice of ½ lime, stirring to combine and fluffing the rice with a fork. Nestle in the meatballs, browned-side up, and cook over low heat, uncovered, for 1 to 2 minutes to warm them. Garnish with the reserved cilantro and Fresno pepper rounds.

lemony skillet chicken with pan croutons

I have a tendency, and maybe we all do, to add more or want to do more. Like, this is good, but should I add something more? And sometimes the answer is no. The less we mess with something, the better it might be. I find that's often true with good ingredients. In this dish, I kept it simple, as I wanted to soak up the irresistible lemony chicken jus with the croutons without having to share it with anything else. You *could* add some mushrooms to the pan, but try it once as is before doing so. Some crumbled feta or Parmesan to sprinkle on top could also be lovely. This dish is one that will please a crowd or a cozy date night, and it's fairly low fuss. Serve with a Bibb salad (page 217) or everyday salad (page 206) to keep things simple.

Serves 4

½ teaspoon red pepper flakes

1 tablespoon Dijon mustard

1 tablespoon soy sauce

2 tablespoons olive oil, plus more for the bread

2 to 2½ pounds bone-in, skin-on chicken thighs or other parts

Salt

2 lemons: 1 thinly sliced into rounds and seeded, 1 halved

½ loaf rustic bread or baguette, torn into bite-size pieces or cubed (2 to 3 cups)

¼ cup packed fresh flat-leaf parsley, leaves and tender stems, gently torn or chopped

Heat the oven to 400°F. In an ovenproof skillet, use a rubber spatula or wooden spoon to mix together the red pepper flakes, mustard, soy sauce, and olive oil until smooth, sliding it across the surface of the pan to blend. Pat the chicken dry and season all over with salt. Add the chicken, turning to coat all over with the mixture and sneaking some under the skin, then set skin-side up in the skillet. Nestle the lemon slices in the pan and pour in ½ cup water. Slide the skillet into the oven and cook for 30 minutes.

Put the bread in a large bowl, drizzle with oil, and lightly season with salt, then toss to coat. Nestle some of the bread pieces into the liquid, some between the chicken pieces, and some on top. Roast for 10 to 12 minutes more, until the chicken is browned on top and the bread is crunchy and crisp. Squeeze a lemon half over everything, then top with the parsley. Cut the remaining lemon half into wedges and serve with the chicken.

note: You can use chicken broth or white wine instead of the water for even more flavor.

citrusy mussels with pickled peppers

At lunch with my friends Ben and Nichole on a sunny NYC day, he and I both ordered mussels. While I dove in, using an empty mussel shell to pluck out the plump meat and pop it in my mouth, I looked over to see him carefully doing the same, but rather than immediately eating them, he put them back into the pot until all were removed from the shell. Only then did he begin to enjoy them. Since this illuminating experience, I've learned that there are others like Ben, and I honestly can't decide which approach I like better. On one hand, the mussels spend more time soaking in the flavorful broth. On the other, the plucking and immediately popping them into your mouth is part of the fun of mussels, and also makes you slow down a bit between each bite. There's no right or wrong, but this can be a conversation topic at your dinner table while you eat these.

Serve 4

1 red onion, thinly sliced

Salt

2 tablespoons olive oil

½ cup drained and sliced peperoncini

2 lemons, cut into rounds, seeded, then into thin strips, or 1 small orange

4 to 6 garlic cloves, thinly sliced

3 pounds mussels, scrubbed and debearded

1 cup white wine, preferably what you're drinking

Crusty bread, for serving

Butter, for serving (optional)

Heat a dry large pot with a tight-fitting lid over medium–high heat until hot, about 2 minutes. Add the onion to the dry pan and season lightly with salt. Cook, undisturbed, for 2 minutes, then stir and cook for 2 minutes more, letting the onions sweat out some of their moisture. Stir in the olive oil and cook, stirring often, until the onions start to soften and shrink, about 4 minutes more. Add the peperoncini, lemon slices, and garlic, cooking until softened in spots and stirring occasionally, about 2 minutes more.

Add the mussels and wine, cover, and adjust the heat to maintain a gentle boil. Cook until most of the mussels have opened, about 5 minutes. Discard any that haven't opened. Serve with bread, buttering it if you'd like, and eating the mussels however you like.

vinegary spring + winter pork chops, 2 ways
asparagus with parsley + feta & parmesan white beans

When I first went to the Little Owl in NYC in my mid-twenties, after fully stalking the reservation line (pre-online bookings, that's how long ago it was), I ordered the pork chop. This might not sound unusual to you, but I had never thought of myself as a pork chop person—until the jolly-looking gentleman next to me began chatting with my friend and me, telling us how he'd tried every pork chop in the city and this was his favorite. (His second favorite, if you're curious, was the pork chop at Union Square Cafe.) Thus my journey into pork chops began. For both the springy and wintery version, you start with the same base, then finish differently for a bright, vegetable-based dish or a cozier one that's more in line with the original dish.

Serves 2

2 bone-in rib or center-cut pork chops, with the fat cap, if it has one, 1¼ to 1½ inches thick, patted dry

Salt and freshly cracked black pepper

2 tablespoons olive oil

Season the pork chops all over with salt and pepper. Heat a dry 12-inch cast-iron or other heavy skillet over medium-high heat until very hot, about 2 minutes. Add the olive oil, then immediately add the pork chops and cook, undisturbed, until they're browned on the bottom and easily release from the pan, 6 to 7 minutes (it's gonna get a bit smoky, so open those windows and turn on the fans).

Flip with tongs, then cook until browned on the other side, about 3 minutes more. Flip again and cook until the center is medium or reaches 145°F, 2 to 4 minutes more, flipping after each minute (thinner ones might be done sooner). Using tongs, hold the chops together and sear the fat caps, if they have them, for 1 minute, then remove and set on a plate in a warm spot to rest.

(cont.)

for the springy version

1 bunch asparagus or Broccolini, ends trimmed (if using Broccolini, cut lengthwise into thin pieces)

¼ to ½ teaspoon red pepper flakes, depending on your heat preference

Salt

Olive oil, as needed

2 teaspoons Dijon mustard

2 tablespoons sherry vinegar or red wine vinegar

2 scallions, thinly sliced

½ cup crumbled feta

¼ cup packed fresh parsley leaves, gently torn or roughly chopped

for the wintery version

1 (15-ounce) can white beans, such as navy, cannellini, or butter, drained and rinsed

½ cup low-sodium chicken broth or vegetable broth, or water

¼ to ½ teaspoon red pepper flakes, depending on your heat preference

Salt

¼ cup grated Parmesan

2 teaspoons Dijon mustard

2 tablespoons balsamic vinegar

¼ cup packed fresh parsley leaves, gently torn or chopped

Freshly ground black pepper

the springy version

Place the same pan over medium-high heat without wiping it out, then add the asparagus. Season with the red pepper flakes and salt and cook until blistered on both sides, 3 to 5 minutes, stirring halfway through (if it looks dry, add a drizzle of oil). In a small bowl, mix together the mustard, vinegar, and scallions. Remove the pan from the heat, then add the mustard mixture to the center of the pan, being careful of the rising steam, and stir until the vinegar bubbles away and the mixture thickens slightly, about 30 seconds. Return the pork chops to the pan, along with any collected juices, turning them to coat, then nestling them in. Top with the feta and parsley and serve.

the wintery version

Place the same pan over medium heat without wiping it out, then add the beans, broth, and red pepper flakes. Season with salt. Cook, stirring occasionally, until the beans are softened and creamy and heated through, 1 to 2 minutes. Stir in half the Parmesan and the mustard, then return the pork chops to the pan, along with any collected juices. Pour the vinegar around the skillet, letting it bubble away until the mixture is thickened with just a little bit of liquid pooling on the surface of the pan, about 1 minute, flipping the chops halfway through. Top with the remaining Parmesan, the parsley, and a few grinds of black pepper.

sheet pan chicken with broccolini, feta + herby peppers

You may agree or agree to disagree when you make this dish, so I'm going to go ahead and say that I find the flavor profile to straddle somewhere between BBQ chicken and, with the lime-pickled chile, a bit of a Southeast Asian profile, so really it's a melting pot of flavors, but one that I think will make you happy. While this recipe calls for bone-in chicken parts, you can easily swap in boneless breasts or thighs; just reduce the cooking time and adjust the Broccolini addition time.

Serves 4

1 (4 to 6-ounce) can tomato paste

2 tablespoons thick full-fat yogurt, such as skyr or Greek yogurt

Salt

1 teaspoon ground cumin

¼ to ½ teaspoon red pepper flakes, depending on your heat preference

3 tablespoons olive oil, divided

2 to 2½ pounds bone-in, skin-on chicken parts

1 jalapeño or Fresno pepper, sliced

Juice of 1 lime

1 bunch Broccolini, ends trimmed, thick stalks halved lengthwise, or 1 small head of broccoli, florets cut into bite-size pieces

½ cup water or low-sodium chicken broth

¼ cup crumbled feta

¼ cup packed fresh cilantro, leaves and tender stems, gently torn or chopped

Heat the oven to 400°F. In a large bowl, combine the tomato paste, yogurt, 1 teaspoon salt, the cumin, red pepper flakes, and 1 tablespoon of the olive oil until pastelike (there won't be a ton). Pat the chicken dry, season all over with salt, then coat with the tomato paste mixture, sneaking some under the skin. Arrange the chicken skin-side up on a sheet pan, rubbing any marinade remaining in the bowl over the tops of the chicken pieces. Bake for 20 minutes.

While the chicken is in the oven, in a small bowl, combine the jalapeño, lime juice, and a generous pinch of salt and toss to combine. Set aside; toss once while the chicken cooks, if you remember.

Remove the sheet pan from the oven and drizzle the remaining 2 tablespoons olive oil in the empty spots on the pan. Dip the Broccolini florets in the oil, coating them, then lay them flat. Add the water or broth to the pan, carefully tilting it so the liquid moves around. Return to the oven and bake until the Broccolini is charred and the chicken cooked through, about 20 minutes more. Top with the feta and cilantro and serve.

sumac-dill salmon with lime herbed rice

One of my favorite things to do is to chop dill, something I watched my grandmother do as she made ghormeh sabzi, a favorite Persian dish of mine chock-full of herbs. Starting with a giant, unruly pile, hearing it crunching beneath my knife, inhaling its aroma, chopping until the mound becomes smaller and smaller—it's utterly satisfying. I also find dill to be a particularly beautiful herb: The frondlike leaves at the top are delicate and feathery, adding a touch of elegance to a dish that I find incredibly attractive. This ended up being way more of a love letter to dill than I intended, and you don't have to feel as strongly about it as I do, but I will say you have to have some love for dill if this recipe is going to make you happy. This recipe uses a lot—as my friend Rebecca said when making this recipe, "You'll know you're using enough dill when you think you're using too much"—but it works out in the end, I promise! This dish goes really well with the lime-ginger radishes (see page 220).

Serves 4

3 tablespoons olive oil

2 teaspoons ground sumac

1 teaspoon ground cumin

½ teaspoon red pepper flakes

2 limes: 1 zested and thinly sliced, 1 cut into wedges

1 large bunch dill, thick stalks trimmed, three-quarters finely chopped, the rest reserved for garnish

Salt

1 (2-pound) fillet of salmon, or 4 (6-ounce) salmon fillets, skin on or off

1 cup basmati rice

Heat the oven to 400°F. In a small bowl or measuring cup, mix the olive oil, sumac, cumin, red pepper flakes, lime zest, and 2 teaspoons of the chopped dill.

Add the salmon to a baking dish or sheet pan, salt it all over, then place skin-side down. Pour the dill oil over the top and sides of the salmon, gently rubbing it in. Surround it with the lime rounds, rubbing them in the oil in the pan and removing any seeds. Let marinate at room temperature while you start on the rice.

In a saucepan with a tight-fitting lid, combine the rice, 2 cups water, and 1 teaspoon salt. Bring the liquid to a boil, then mix in the remaining chopped dill, cover, and reduce the heat to maintain a simmer. Cook until the rice is tender and most of the liquid has evaporated, 8 to 12 minutes more (you can peek under to check, just not too often please!). Squeeze the juice of 2 lime wedges into the rice, fluffing it with a fork, cover, and set aside for 5 minutes.

After you start the rice, roast the salmon until just cooked through in the middle, 12 to 17 minutes, depending on the thickness of the salmon (thinner fillets will be closer to 12 minutes, while 1- to 1½-inch-thick pieces will be closer to 17 minutes). Squeeze one of the lime wedges over the salmon. Garnish with the reserved dill and serve with the rice and remaining lime wedges.

chicken thighs with burst tomatoes + croutons

There are many things I love about food, so I don't want to say this is my favorite thing ever, but I truly and deeply love soaking bread in soup or sauce. The ideal piece of bread can both hold its shape and soak up the flavorful liquid pooling at the bottom of a bowl. These croutons, scattered on the sheet pan during the last bit of cooking, achieve this duality: Pieces nestled in the tomato-and-chicken jus are drenched with flavor, while the parts sitting a bit above become crunchy and crisp. The jammy tomatoes and steamy garlic cloves are ideal for spreading on both the chicken and croutons (pop the garlic out of the peel to spread it). You could also peel and smash the garlic, instead, at the start of the recipe.

Serves 4

1 teaspoon red pepper flakes

2 teaspoons dried oregano

2 teaspoons Dijon mustard

1 tablespoon sherry vinegar or red wine vinegar

¼ cup olive oil, divided

2 pints grape tomatoes or cherry tomatoes

4 or 5 garlic cloves, unpeeled (excess skin rubbed off)

Salt

2 pounds bone-in, skin-on chicken parts, such as legs, drumsticks, or thighs

½ medium loaf country, sourdough, or rustic bread or classic French baguette, torn into bite-size pieces or cubed (about 3 cups)

¼ cup fresh basil or parsley leaves, gently torn or chopped

¼ cup grated Parmesan

Heat the oven to 400°F. In a large bowl, combine the red pepper flakes, oregano, mustard, vinegar, and 2 tablespoons of the olive oil until smooth. Put the tomatoes and garlic on a sheet pan, season lightly with salt, and pour in a quarter of the marinade, then toss to combine. Pat the chicken dry, season all over with salt, then add to the bowl and coat with the mixture, sneaking some under the skin, too. Place the chicken skin-side up on the sheet pan, surrounding it with the tomatoes and garlic. Roast for 30 minutes.

In a large bowl, toss the bread with the remaining 2 tablespoons olive oil and season lightly with salt. Scatter the bread over the sheet pan and bake until the bread is crisp and crunchy, the tomatoes burst, and the chicken is browned and cooked through, with the juices running clear when pierced with a fork, 12 to 15 minutes more. Scatter the herbs and Parmesan over everything and serve.

caponata-ish skillet eggplant with tomato

This eggplant dish is similar in many ways to Sicilian caponata, but with a few twists. Think of it as one that is forgiving about the size you cut things and what you put in, as long as they are more or less in the same family of flavors. Definitely add more spice in the form of red pepper flakes if you want, or toss in a chopped fresh jalapeño with the garlic. Pickled jalapeño or peperoncini would also be welcome to add a bit more heat and acidity. A generous sprinkling of feta wouldn't make anyone unhappy, either, though Parmesan would also be a nice companion. Over time, it will firm up and become more caponata-like, so you can definitely make it ahead to serve cold the next day, which also gives the flavors even more time to hang out and bond. Bring it to a picnic or potluck, or snack on it throughout the week. Please eat this with bread—it's how both you and the dish will be happiest.

Serves 4 to 6

2 large or 3 small Italian eggplants, trimmed and cut into ½-inch cubes (4 to 5 cups)

1 medium red onion, thinly sliced

Salt

3 tablespoons olive oil

½ cup pitted green olives, such as Castelvetrano, roughly chopped

1 (12-ounce) jar roasted red peppers, drained and sliced

3 or 4 garlic cloves, peeled, smashed, and roughly chopped

1 tablespoon ground turmeric

1 tablespoon ground cumin

1 tablespoon piménton (smoked paprika)

1 (28-ounce) can crushed tomatoes

¼ cup packed fresh basil or cilantro leaves, gently torn or chopped

Crusty bread, for serving

Heat a dry 12-inch cast-iron or other heavy skillet over medium-high heat until very hot, about 2 minutes. Add the eggplant and onion to the dry pan, season lightly with salt, and spread in an even layer (the pan will be crowded, and that's fine). Cook, undisturbed, for 2 minutes, then stir and cook, undisturbed, for 2 minutes more. Stir and repeat, until the eggplant is browned and charred in spots (so much good flavor!) and the moisture released by both the eggplant and onion has evaporated, about 2 minutes more. Lower the heat if the onion threatens to burn.

Add the olive oil and stir to combine, then add the olives and cook until they start to blister in spots, about 4 minutes more. Add the roasted peppers, garlic, turmeric, cumin, and paprika and cook, stirring, until fragrant, about 30 seconds more. Pour in the tomatoes, then fill the can halfway with water and add it to the pot. Season lightly with salt and bring the liquid to a boil, then reduce the heat to maintain a simmer, with small bubbles forming but not splattering red splotches all over your kitchen (lower the heat if this happens or partially cover the skillet). Cook until the tomato sauce is thick and more stew-like than sauce-like and the eggplant is silky and broken down, 35 to 45 minutes, or let this simmer on very low for as long as you need. Top with the basil and serve with crusty bread.

sheet pan mediterranean nachos
(with feta + olives)

I think there's something so enjoyable about eating this way, whether for dinner, snacking, or sharing plates. While I love more traditional nachos, I tend to lean more to this flavor profile, which means it's essentially all my favorite snacking foods on one giant plate. It looks like a lot of ingredients, but please forge ahead as you're mostly piling a ton of delicious ingredients on top of each other. Pita chips can be made one of two ways: Either peel apart the two layers of the pita for thinner chips, or keep them as is for thicker ones. Here we're going for thicker chips that can hold up to the toppings.

Serves 4

5 large pitas (about 6 inches in diameter)

3 tablespoons olive oil, divided, plus more as needed

Salt

1 (15-ounce) can white beans, such as cannellini or navy, drained and rinsed

1 cup thick full-fat yogurt, such as Greek yogurt or skyr, or labneh

Juice of 1 small lemon

¼ cup packed fresh parsley or cilantro, leaves and tender stems, roughly chopped, plus some sprigs, gently torn, for garnish

½ teaspoon ground cumin

¾ cup crumbled feta

2 cups Castelvetrano or other meaty olives, pitted and smashed (see page 67)

2 to 4 tablespoons harissa, depending on your heat preference (you can serve this on the side, too)

1 teaspoon ground sumac or za'atar, for sprinkling

Flaky sea salt

2 tablespoons packed fresh dill, gently torn or chopped

Heat the oven to 400°F. Use shears to cut the pita in quarters, then cut each in half one last time so you have 8 wedges. Spread them over a sheet pan and drizzle with 2 tablespoons of the olive oil, adding more as needed so they all have a light coating (they won't be perfectly coated all over, which is fine), then season lightly with salt.

Put the beans on another sheet pan, drizzle with the remaining 1 tablespoon olive oil, and season lightly with salt, then toss to combine. Bake until the pita wedges are crispy and browned and the beans warmed, 10 to 12 minutes. (If you have the energy, flip the pita wedges halfway through, but I'm always too lazy to do this, and it's fine; note that they will continue to brown out of the oven.) Let cool slightly along with the beans.

Meanwhile, in a small bowl, mix the yogurt, lemon juice, chopped parsley, and cumin until the juice is incorporated. Stir in ½ cup of the feta.

On a large serving platter or two large plates, create a layer of pita chips. Top with half the feta, half the beans, and half the olives, and use a spoon to create small piles of yogurt around the pita chips. Repeat with another layer of chips, making it narrower so that it creates a small platform in the center, then add the remaining toppings. Dollop some harissa here and there, depending on your heat preference. Sprinkle everything with the sumac, some flaky salt, the dill, and the parsley sprigs, and serve warm.

roasted mustard salmon with hint-of-mint escarole salad

When I first moved to Miami in the brutal heat of August, I would go to an early dinner at Macchialina, a 10-minute walk from my apartment, to escape. I love a good solo meal at the bar, and this escarole salad was often my companion: the bitter greens doused in a generous amount of dressing, with just a hint of mint. It popped up every fourth bite or so, just long enough for you to forget it's there and then be pleasantly surprised by its fresh, invigorating taste. This salad uses both raw and cooked escarole from the sheet pan, plus the crunchy croutons that cooked with it, serving the salmon on the side.

Serves 4

4 anchovies, patted dry and snipped with shears or chopped into small pieces

3 lemons: 2 juiced, 1 halved

1 tablespoon Dijon mustard

½ medium loaf thick, crusty bread, or ¼ classic French baguette, torn into bite-size pieces (2 to 3 cups)

1 bunch escarole, ends trimmed

2 tablespoons olive oil, plus more for the bread and escarole

Salt

4 (4- to 6-ounce) salmon fillets, skin on or off

¼ cup fresh mint leaves, finely chopped

¼ cup unsalted and roasted pistachios, roughly chopped

2 tablespoons grated Parmesan

Freshly ground black pepper

Heat the oven to 400°F. In a large serving bowl, combine the anchovies, lemon juice, and mustard, using a fork to mash the anchovy bits and mix them with the rest until it's smooth-ish.

Spread the bread over a sheet pan and add half the escarole, tearing it into small pieces as you add it. Drizzle lightly with olive oil and season lightly with salt, and toss so everything is coated with a slight sheen. Push to sides of the sheet pan, creating a gap in the center. Season the salmon with salt all over, set skin-side down in the middle of the pan, then spoon some of the mustard mixture on top of each fillet, rubbing it over the tops and sides.

Bake until the croutons are crisp and the salmon is just cooked through in the center, 12 to 17 minutes, depending on the thickness of the salmon (12 minutes for thinner cuts, up to 17 minutes for 1½-inch-thick center-cut pieces.)

While the salmon cooks, add the 2 tablespoons olive oil to the serving bowl with the remaining mustard mixture and whisk until smooth. Chop the remaining escarole into small ribbons, then add it to the dressing in the bowl. Add the mint and pistachios and toss to combine. Set aside until the salmon is done.

Squeeze a lemon half over the salmon and cut the remaining half into wedges for serving. Add the cooked escarole, croutons, and Parmesan to the salad bowl and toss to combine. Season as needed with salt and lemon, and finish with a few grinds of pepper, and serve together.

tip: If you don't like anchovies, you can substitute 1 tablespoon white miso instead.

lemony ginger chicken with potatoes + onions

This is a warming, cozy dish, with flavors reminiscent of the health shots I often take when I feel a cold coming on, so it's perfect for chilly nights or if you feel like you need a little pick-me-up dinner. Some, aka my friend Jennifer, might call it an elixir-like broth. Slowly cooking in a bath of zingy ginger and lemon juice along with the potatoes and onions, the chicken becomes falling-off-the-bone tender with minimal work from you once it's in the oven. Topped with lightly dressed herbs, it's easy enough to make for yourself but fancy enough to serve guests.

Serves 4

½ teaspoon ground turmeric

2 teaspoons grated fresh ginger (from a 2-inch piece)

½ teaspoon red pepper flakes

Freshly cracked black pepper

Zest and juice of 2 lemons

3 tablespoons olive oil, divided

2 to 2½ pounds bone-in, skin-on chicken parts, such as whole legs, thighs, and/or drumsticks

Salt

1 pound baby potatoes, large ones halved

1 small red or yellow onion, cut into 1-inch-thick wedges

2 cups low-sodium chicken broth or vegetable broth

½ cup fresh cilantro, leaves and tender stems, gently torn or chopped

¼ cup fresh dill, leaves and tender stems, gently torn or chopped

Crusty bread or cooked rice, for serving

Heat the oven to 400°F. In a 9 x 13-inch baking dish, combine the turmeric, ginger, red pepper flakes, a few grinds of black pepper, the lemon zest, and 2 tablespoons of the olive oil. Pat the chicken dry and season it all over with salt, then coat it all over with the turmeric mixture, lifting up the skin and tucking some under, if you feel comfortable doing that.

Set the chicken skin-side up in the baking dish and surround it with the potatoes and onion, then pour in the lemon juice and broth, turning the potatoes and onion to coat them in the liquid. Top with a few grinds of black pepper. Cover the pan with foil and bake for 45 minutes. Carefully uncover and bake for 30 minutes more, so the tops of the chicken pieces brown. Let cool for 5 to 10 minutes.

Meanwhile, in a small serving bowl, combine the cilantro and dill. Set aside. Just before serving, toss the herbs with the remaining 1 tablespoon olive oil, seasoning lightly with salt. Top the chicken with some of the herbs and serve with bread and the remaining herbs on the side.

harissa-poached salmon with tomatoes

A whole fillet of salmon is always a beautiful centerpiece, and with this one-dish technique, it cooks in the oven while you set the table, make a salad, like the cucumber-and-mint salad on page 202, and pour the wine. Crushed green olives would be a lovely addition to the cooking liquid to give it a briny depth and some texture (if you use them, reduce the salt to ¼ teaspoon). Serve in shallow bowls with bread or rice to soak up the liquid.

Serves 4

½ to 1 tablespoon harissa, depending on your heat preference

½ teaspoon piménton (smoked paprika)

1 tablespoon soy sauce

1 cup white wine, preferably what you're drinking

½ cup olive oil

2 pints cherry tomatoes or grape tomatoes

1 (15-ounce) can white beans, such as cannellini or navy, drained and rinsed (optional)

Salt and freshly cracked black pepper

1 (2-pound) salmon fillet, or 4 (4- to 6-ounce) thick center-cut fillets, skin on or off

¼ cup packed fresh parsley, leaves and tender stems, roughly torn

Cooked rice or bread, for serving

Heat the oven to 400°F. In a shallow 9 by 13-inch baking dish or braising dish with a lid, mix together the harissa, paprika, soy sauce, wine, and olive oil. Stir in the tomatoes and the beans (if using) and season with ½ teaspoon salt. Gently pierce the tomatoes with the tip of a sharp knife so they burst and release their juices while cooking.

Add the salmon to the baking dish, turning it to coat in the liquid, then set it skin-side down, spoon some more liquid over it, and season lightly with salt and pepper. Cover with foil and bake for 25 minutes, for the salmon to just be cooked through. Remove the foil carefully (it will be steamy), then let cool for 5 minutes. Top with the parsley and serve with rice or bread.

dad's kebabs

One evening many years ago, a cat wandered into my parents' yard while they were having dinner. My dad left her little pieces of the kebab they were eating, and she came back the next night and so on. Eventually, this cat found her way into their home, and after taking her to the vet for a checkup, they learned that there was a reason she was so hungry: She was very, very pregnant. In our basement she gave birth to five kittens, all of which found loving homes, and she earned the nickname, the kebab. We like to joke that my dad's kebabs won her heart and her trust, so I hope they win yours, too.

That being said, this recipe is not technically a kebab, as I skip the skewers, but if you like, you can use metal or wooden ones (just soak them so they don't burn). As you shape the kebabs, you'll realize that this might not be the most photo-worthy meal, but you can always cut them up into chunks after cooking. Serve as is or with some yogurt with a little bit of lime and salt added to it.

Serves 4

1 pint grape tomatoes or cherry tomatoes

1 red onion: ½ thinly sliced, ½ grated and extra liquid pressed out with a paper towel

2 tablespoons olive oil

Salt

1 tablespoon ground turmeric

1 tablespoon ground cumin

¼ teaspoon red pepper flakes

Freshly cracked black pepper

1 pound 80/20 ground beef

Ground sumac, or 1 lime, halved

½ cup crumbled feta, for serving

¼ cup fresh mint leaves, for serving

Toasted or warmed pita, for serving

Heat the broiler to high with a rack 6 inches from the heat source.

On a sheet pan, mix together the tomatoes, sliced onions, and olive oil, seasoning lightly with salt. In a large bowl, combine the grated onion, turmeric, cumin, red pepper flakes, 1 teaspoon salt, and a few grinds of black pepper, then add the ground beef and mix until it's all a mustardy color (wear gloves if you don't want stained fingers). Divide the beef into 8 equal-size chunks, then wet your hands with water so the meat won't stick. Place one piece in the flat of your palm and form it into an oblong sausage-like shape with your fingers, as if you were skewering it. I find it helps to use the fingers of the hand holding it to press down to lengthen and shape it as it rests in my palm (don't judge it by its look here). Place the shaped beef in the center of the sheet pan as you work, turning it over to coat with the oil.

Broil until the tops are browned, about 4 minutes (keep an eye on it), then flip the beef and move the tomatoes around, rotating the pan in the oven. Cook until the other side is browned and the meat is cooked through, with no pink remaining, about 3 minutes more, depending on the strength of your broiler. Sprinkle sumac or the lime juice on the kebabs. Serve with the feta and mint in small bowls and the pitas alongside.

some thoughts on our friend polenta

One of the things I love most about sitting at a restaurant bar is getting to chat with random people. I particularly love going solo, as this usually sets you up better to speak to the people passing by. Becoming a regular is even better, as you get to know the staff and see the quirks of other diners and regulars. For example, one night at the bar at Macchialina, an older gentleman came in for his pickup order of "creamy polenta, no toppings." Now, the polenta is fantastic there, there's no doubt about that. But I loved that he eschewed the equally delicious ragu on top of it, just for the polenta. When we started chatting, he explained that he loved eating it like porridge—he wasn't one of those people who cuts it up to fry or grill it. Oh no, he likes it creamy, sometimes with a fried egg on top for breakfast. I truly liked this man. He was a man of conviction and decision. He had many other thoughts about polenta, which he shared, like how he sometimes makes it with Gorgonzola and so on, though he quickly dismissed my Parmesan input—"Too salty." Imagine, if I had just sat alone at a table or ordered delivery, I would never have met this gem of a man and had some solid chat about polenta.

Now, on to the actual business of polenta.

I was late to the home-cooking polenta game because in my mind, I saw it as a lot of work—near constant stirring and watching? No, no, no. While this recipe is fairly easy, I will say that this is not your restaurant polenta: creamy and akin to mashed potatoes, lush, rich, and smooth in texture. That polenta, while utterly delicious, is best left to restaurants and eaten only occasionly because it likely includes much more cheese/butter/oil than I would be able to knowingly serve someone.

This one has a soft, plump, porridgelike texture, which I love to eat piping hot, topped with a tomato sauce (even better with meatballs and tomato sauce, see page 190, or chicken with peppers and onions on page 164). Think of it loosely as an alternative to rice or pasta when you want something filling on the side, knowing that this is best with something a bit saucy—a simple skillet egg (page 13) also works! Some cooked vegetables with a generous drizzle of oil to finish everything off are also a great idea.

While this dish hails from Northern Italy and can be made even creamier and more luscious in many ways, this is a variation inspired by the original, so please don't be upset with me for straying from tradition.

Serves 4

1 teaspoon salt, plus more as needed

1 cup polenta

2 tablespoons olive oil, plus more if needed

½ cup grated Parmesan or Pecorino Romano (a bit saltier and stronger) cheese, plus more as needed

Red pepper flakes

Bring 3½ cups water and the salt to a boil in a large Dutch oven or heavy-bottomed pot. Use a wooden spoon to slowly stir in the polenta. Cook, stirring, until the mixture comes to a boil, then reduce the heat to low and cook, stirring every minute or so to prevent large bubbles popping, until it becomes a cohesive mixture and thickens, and the grains start to soften, about 8 minutes. You should feel some resistance as you stir, but if it feels like you're really needing to use some arm muscle, add a splash of water to loosen it.

Stir in the olive oil, the Parmesan, and some red pepper flakes (use anywhere from a pinch up to ½ teaspoon, depending on your heat preference), until combined. Cook, stirring every few minutes to make sure nothing is stuck to the bottom and adding more water as needed to maintain a smooth and creamy consistency, until you don't taste any individual grains when biting into it, 10 to 15 minutes more. Season to taste with more salt or cheese, as desired. You can always finish it with a drizzle of olive oil for a smoother texture.

variation: Stir in ¼ to ½ cup crumbled Gorgonzola like our bar friend.

skillet chicken with peppers + onions

With a distinctively fajita-like flavoring, this chicken can be cooked bone-in, bone-in, or boneless (see below). It cooks slowly in the oven so you can spend your time focusing on the polenta, which is the perfect creamy counterpart to the silky onions and slightly spicy sauce. Chipotle peppers in adobo are typically smoked jalapeños with a lot of spices, so you can increase the amount of sauce and number of peppers used, depending on your heat preference. Freeze any leftover chipotles and adobo in small pouches to use as needed.

Serves 4

1 teaspoon ground cumin

1 teaspoon piménton (smoked paprika)

Salt

1 or 2 canned chipotle peppers in adobo sauce, depending on heat preference, roughly chopped, plus 1 tablespoon sauce from the can

1 tablespoon soy sauce

1½ to 2 pounds bone-in, skin-on chicken parts, such as drumsticks, thighs, and/or wings

1 red onion, thinly sliced

2 red or orange bell peppers, seeded and thinly sliced

1 head garlic (or less, if desired), broken up into individual cloves, still in their peels, rubbed to remove excess skin

2 tablespoons olive oil, plus more as needed

1 lime, cut into wedges

¼ cup fresh cilantro, leaves and tender stems

1 Fresno pepper or jalapeño, sliced into rounds (optional)

Cooked polenta (see page 163), cooked rice, or tortillas, for serving

Heat the oven to 400°F. In a large bowl, mix together the cumin, paprika, ½ teaspoon salt, the chipotle(s) and adobo, and the soy sauce. Pat the chicken dry, then add it to the mixture, turning to coat all over and sneaking some under the skin, if you feel confident doing so.

In a 12-inch cast-iron or other ovenproof skillet, combine the onion, bell peppers, and garlic cloves, season lightly with salt, then drizzle with the olive oil and stir to coat. Lay the chicken skin-side up on top of the onion and peppers. Transfer to the oven and roast until the peppers and onion are silky soft and the chicken is cooked through and browned on the outside, about 45 minutes. This would be a good time make your polenta or rice, if doing so.

Squeeze 2 lime wedges over the chicken, then top with the cilantro and Fresno pepper, if using. Spoon the chicken, peppers, and onions on top of the polenta and serve the remaining lime wedges on the side. Squeeze the garlic cloves out of their little pouches and slather on the polenta or on tortillas.

for skinless, boneless thighs: Use the same amount of chicken. Cook the onions and peppers for 25 minutes, then stir, and top with the chicken. Cook for 20 minutes more, or until the chicken is cooked through.

stew-ish chicken with tomato, peppers + onions

While staying in an apartment overlooking the sea in the northern part of Menorca, I woke up at 2 a.m. to a loud crash. Fully freaked out, I tiptoed out of the bedroom to see the chair on the patio knocked over and a strong wind rattling the windows—it's an island known for its strong wind and storms. I clumsily closed the storm shutters in the dark with the rain pounding down on me and slid back into bed, feeling like I was having an *Under the Tuscan Sun* moment when all the things start to fall apart in the house (there was also minor flooding). The next morning, the previously calm and flat sea was full of whitecaps, and, while it wasn't the ideal sunny day, it was ideal cooking weather, perfect for making this warm and cozy chicken dish. It's a good one to make for when you want to leave something simmering on the stove while you putter around, wearing fuzzy socks, reading a book, and enjoying the aroma wafting through the house.

Serves 4

1 tablespoon ground cumin

1 tablespoon piménton (smoked paprika)

Salt

¼ cup olive oil, divided

2 pounds bone-in, skin-on chicken parts, such as thighs, drumsticks, or breasts, excess skin and fat trimmed

1 (28-ounce) can crushed tomatoes

1 (4 to 6-ounce) tube or can tomato paste

1 medium red onion, halved, then quartered (to make 8 wedges total)

2 red bell peppers, seeded and thinly sliced

4 garlic cloves, peeled and smashed

1 (15-ounce) can chickpeas, drained and rinsed

2 tablespoons red wine, preferably what you're drinking, or sherry vinegar

Freshly ground black pepper

2 cups baby arugula or spinach, for serving

Crusty bread, toasted pita, or cooked rice, for serving

In a large bowl, mix together the cumin, paprika, 1 teaspoon salt, and 2 tablespoons of the olive oil. Pat the chicken dry, then coat all over with the spice mixture, sneaking some under the skin.

Heat the remaining 2 tablespoons olive oil in a large Dutch oven or lidded pot over medium-high heat until shimmering. Add the chicken, skin-side down—the pot will be crowded, and that's okay. Cook, undisturbed, for 5 minutes, until the skin starts to color, then flip over. Meanwhile, in the bowl you used for the chicken, mix together the crushed tomatoes, tomato paste, and 1½ cups room-temperature water.

Add the onion, bell peppers, garlic, chickpeas, tomato-water mixture, and wine to the pot. Season lightly with salt and stir as best you can. Cover, raise the heat to high, and bring to a boil, then reduce the heat to maintain a gentle simmer, with small bubbles popping up. Cook, covered, until everything is soft and the meat is falling-off-the-bone tender, about 45 minutes, stirring once halfway through and making sure the heat remains low so nothing sticks on the bottom.

Uncover and cook for 15 minutes more to let some of the liquid evaporate and thicken the rest—you can raise the heat a little here if it's not really bubbling, but avoid intense bubbles so the chicken stays tender. Season to taste with salt and black pepper.

If desired, place a handful of arugula in the bottom of each bowl and spoon the stew on top. Finish with a few arugula leaves and a generous grind of black pepper. (Remove the chicken skin if it bothers you.) Serve with crusty bread, toasted pita, or rice to soak it all up.

autumnal cider-braised chicken with apples

"Autumnal" is such a fun word, isn't it? That time of year when the humidity is replaced by a crispness in the air, a hint of cool, cold weather so you know what's coming ahead, but you still have some time to enjoy this seasonal change. Living in New York, it was also the time for a weekend escape to go apple picking, wandering around orchards, plucking apples from the trees that weren't fully picked over yet. In my mind, it was always more fun than the reality. I usually came home with way too many apples and quickly lost motivation to make apple butter and applesauce as I had intended. But I do love the cider. Whether you buy a jug of that at the orchard and simply watch others pick apples or get it at a grocery store, pour a little in this skillet to flavor the chicken and spike the rest with some rum to drink while you wait for it to cook.

Serves 4

2 teaspoons white miso paste

2 teaspoons ground cumin

2 teaspoons grated or minced fresh ginger (from a 2-inch piece)

¼ teaspoon red pepper flakes

3 tablespoons olive oil, divided

2 to 2½ pounds bone-in, skin-on chicken thighs (4 to 6 pieces)

Salt

2 apples, preferably Pink Lady, Honeycrisp, or Gala, cored and cut into 1-inch-thick wedges

½ cup apple cider or unsweetened apple juice

Juice of 1 small lemon, or 2 tablespoons apple cider vinegar

2 tablespoons packed fresh parsley, leaves and tender stems, gently torn or chopped

In a large bowl, mash together the miso, cumin, ginger, red pepper flakes, and 1 tablespoon of the olive oil. Pat the chicken dry, season all over with salt, then coat with the mixture, sneaking some under the skin.

Heat 1 tablespoon oil in a 12-inch cast-iron skillet over medium-high heat, tilting it to coat the skillet, until shimmering. Add the chicken, skin-side down, and cook until the skin is browned and easily releases from the pan, 5 to 7 minutes. (Keep checking the skin and move the pieces around if the spices are getting too dark.)

After you add the chicken to the skillet, add the remaining 1 tablespoon oil to the bowl it was in, mixing to incorporate any remaining spice rub, then add the apples and season lightly with salt. Use tongs to flip the chicken and cook for 2 minutes more, then transfer to a plate. Add the apples and cook, undisturbed, until they shrink down a little, about 2 minutes more.

Pour in the cider and lemon juice, stirring to combine and mix the apples, then return the chicken pieces to the pan, skin-side up, along with any collected juices, pushing the apples to the sides so the chicken has contact with the pan. Adjust the heat to maintain a gentle simmer. Cover and simmer until the chicken is cooked through, 18 to 20 minutes. Stir the fruit around, then increase the heat to medium-high and cook, uncovered, for 5 minutes to let the liquid reduce a little bit more. Spoon some of the juices on top of the chicken, then top with the parsley and serve.

skillet eggplant lasagna

One night in Menorca, I sat in this beautiful courtyard, listening to the birds chirp, the wind rustle the leaves of the trees, and it would have been pretty fantastic other than the fact that I was the only one dining there. Not another soul in sight. I was sipping some white wine, thinking that I had made a giant mistake, but then my main dish arrived. It was a take on eggplant parmigiana but using Mahón cheese, which is made on the tiny island (though it can be found around the world). Any doubt I had was erased as I devoured the entire dish, oblivious to the fact that I was dining alone in a dimly lit courtyard, with the staff probably wondering, *Who is this random girl? It's me!*

Serves 4

1 large Italian eggplant (about 1½ pounds), ends trimmed, cut into ¼-inch-thick rounds

Salt

2 large garlic cloves, grated or minced

1 teaspoon dried oregano

½ to 1 teaspoon red pepper flakes, depending on your heat preference

2 tablespoons plus 1 cup grated Parmesan

1 (28-ounce) can crushed tomatoes

1 tablespoon olive oil

2 handfuls of baby spinach

⅓ pound Mahón, Gouda, cheddar, or pecorino cheese, coarsely grated (about 1⅓ heaping cups), plus more as desired for the final topping layer

¼ cup fresh basil, leaves and tender stems, gently torn or chopped

Crusty bread, for serving (optional, but let's be serious, you're gonna want to scoop that sauce up)

Heat the broiler to high with a rack 6 inches from the heat source. Lay the eggplant slices on a sheet pan (it's okay if some overlap) and sprinkle lightly with salt. Broil until browned on top and dry looking with almost no steam coming out, 5 to 6 minutes. Use tongs to flip the eggplant over and cook until the other side is browned, 3 to 5 minutes more, depending on the thickness of the slices and the strength of your broiler.

While the eggplant cooks, add the garlic, oregano, red pepper flakes, ½ teaspoon salt, and 2 tablespoons of the Parmesan to the can of crushed tomatoes and stir together thoroughly.

Heat the oven to 400°F. Pour the olive oil into a 12-inch cast-iron or other ovenproof skillet and swirl to coat the bottom of the pan, then spoon in about one-third of the tomato mixture and spread it evenly across the bottom. Add half the eggplant in an even layer and a handful of spinach on top. Spoon another third of the tomato mixture on top of the spinach, followed by half the Mahón cheese, adding any chunks that might have fallen while grating, then layer on half the Parmesan. Add a layer of the remaining eggplant, top with another handful of spinach, then spread the remaining tomato mixture on top. Finish with the remaining Parmesan and Mahón cheeses, spreading them to fully cover the top.

Cover with a tight-fitting lid or foil and roast for 25 minutes on the middle rack. Uncover and cook until bubbling and the liquid has reduced, about 15 minutes more. Let sit for 5 minutes to cool, then top with the basil leaves and a sprinkle of red pepper flakes, if desired, and serve with crusty bread.

baked tomato mac 'n' cheese
(aka *sunday supper heaven*)

The first time I made mac 'n' cheese felt like the first time I made a piecrust in the seventh grade. I literally shouted, "You're going to use *that much* butter?!" I was horrified. You have to remember that I grew up in a high-cholesterol household, as it's genetic for my mom and me, and butter felt like the enemy. I felt similarly about the amount of cheese used in traditional mac 'n' cheese.

So this recipe is not your average mac 'n' cheese, as I tried to reduce it as best I could while still keeping it delicious, though there is still a good amount in here. I also added some harissa, fresh tomatoes, and lots of labneh to give it that creamy, lush texture and a few different cheeses to give it tangy, salty contrasts. This rich, cozy one-pot dish is prime for cold, blustery nights when you want to be warmed inside and out, snuggle with loved ones, sip some wine, and forget the impending week.

Serves 4 to 6

Salt

1 pound tubular pasta, such as elbows, cavatappi, fusilli, or small shells

2 tablespoons olive oil, plus more for drizzling

1 (4 to 6-ounce) tube tomato paste (about ½ cup), preferably double-concentrated

2 teaspoons harissa, or 1 teaspoon piménton (smoked paprika)

1 pint grape tomatoes or cherry tomatoes, halved

4 to 8 ounces grated white cheddar, depending on your cheesy desire

4 ounces grated Gruyère

1 cup labneh or drained thick full-fat Greek yogurt

¼ cup panko bread crumbs

½ cup grated Parmesan

¼ teaspoon red pepper flakes

Heat the oven to 400°F. Bring a 12-inch ovenproof braising dish or Dutch oven filled with well-salted water to a boil. Add the pasta and cook until just shy of al dente (it should still be a little too tough to bite through), 2 to 3 minutes less than the package instructions. Reserve 1 cup of the pasta water. Drain the pasta in a colander in the sink, drizzle with olive oil, and toss, then leave it there.

Wipe out the pot and set it over medium-high heat. Add the olive oil and heat until shimmering. Add the tomato paste, harissa, and tomatoes, season lightly with salt, and cook, stirring occasionally, until a deep red color, about 2 minutes.

Reduce the heat to low, add the reserved 1 cup pasta water, the cheddar, Gruyère, and labneh, and stir until no white streaks of yogurt remain (it will look loose and sloppy, totally fine!). Pour in the pasta and stir to coat until all the noodles are a pinkish-red color. It will still look a little soupy at the edges, which you want so the noodles soak up the sauce.

Mix the bread crumbs, Parmesan, and red pepper flakes in a measuring cup, then sprinkle the mixture all over the pasta. Bake until the top and edges are crisp, about 25 minutes. Let cool for 5 to 10 minutes, then scoop out and serve.

stewed chicken with red wine + prunes

My dad, an excellent cook, thoroughly surprised me one night when I was visiting him. Casually, he mentioned that he had made a curry and was going to heat some up as part of our dinner spread. This curry blew my mind. The rich sauce, sweetened by slowly cooked prunes, almost tasted like it had the sweet-sour flavor of tamarind paste, with a pleasant thickness that layered beautifully over rice. I immediately peppered him with questions, and patiently, as always, he recited his steps. This is my version of that memorable dish.

While I find prunes to be irresistibly delicious when cooked, as they have an almost melt-in-your-mouth texture and a savory sweetness, I'd be wary of eating more than four or five in one sitting, for safety's sake. Please be strong and warn your guests, too.

Serve 4

2 tablespoons olive oil

1 yellow onion, diced

Salt

1 teaspoon paprika

1 teaspoon ground turmeric

1 teaspoon ground cumin

1 teaspoon ground oregano

1 teaspoon grated or minced fresh ginger (from a 1-inch piece)

¼ to ½ teaspoon red pepper flakes

2 pounds bone-in, skin-on chicken parts, or 2 Cornish hens

2 tablespoons tomato paste

1½ cups pitted prunes (about 8 ounces)

½ cup good-quality red wine, preferably what you're drinking

2 cups low-sodium chicken broth or water

¼ cup packed fresh parsley, leaves and tender stems, roughly chopped (optional)

Bread or cooked rice, for serving

Heat the olive oil in a Dutch oven or a large pot with a lid over medium-high heat until shimmering. Add the onion, season lightly with salt, and cook until just softened, about 4 minutes. Add the paprika, turmeric, cumin, oregano, ginger, and red pepper flakes and cook, stirring, until fragrant, about 1 minute more. Move the onions to the outskirts of the pot, creating a center stage, and add the chicken skin-side down. Season the exposed part with salt. Cook until the chicken is browned on the bottom and easily releases from the pan, 5 to 7 minutes, stirring the onions every couple of minutes.

Use tongs to turn the chicken over and season the other side with salt, then squeeze the tomato paste over the onions and add the prunes, stirring them around as best you can. Cook until the tomato paste starts to darken in color, about 2 minutes more. Pour in the wine and cook until it bubbles away so that it looks more like a burgundy-colored paste than a loose liquid, about 1½ minutes. Pour in the broth and raise the heat to reach a gentle boil, then cover and lower the heat to maintain a simmer.

Cook for about 45 minutes, checking every so often to make sure it's gently simmering and bubbling. Uncover, spoon some liquid over the chicken, and cook until the sauce has thickened and chicken is cooked through, about 15 minutes more. Season as needed with salt, top with the parsley, if using, and serve with bread.

orecchiette + broccoli rabe soup
(with garlicky bread crumbs)

This particular dish is inspired by an Italian friend who took over my kitchen one night, making me a variation of this, telling me about how he would try to sneak into the kitchen to watch his grandmother make it (cute!).

I love this recipe because I find that everything is soft and tender, something I can easily eat with a spoon, and it feels, in my mind, like it's easy to digest and good to make when I want something filling but not overly spiced. You can also make it with a head of broccoli instead (see note).

Serves 4

3 tablespoons olive oil, divided

½ cup panko bread crumbs

Salt

3 or 4 garlic cloves, grated or minced

1 (32-ounce) can low-sodium chicken broth (4 cups)

1 pound orecchiette

2 bunches broccoli rabe, leaves and florets separated, thick stalks cut off and leaves sliced (roughly 3-inch pieces)

¼ teaspoon red pepper flakes, plus more for serving

4 or 5 oil-packed anchovies (use the remaining anchovies in escarole salad, page 154, or garlicky shrimp pasta, page 124)

¾ cup grated Pecorino Romano or Parmesan, plus more for serving

1 lemon, halved

Heat 1 tablespoon of the olive oil in a large skillet over medium-high heat until shimmering. Add the bread crumbs, season lightly with salt, and stir to coat in the oil. Cook, stirring often, until they start to brown, about 2 minutes, then add half the garlic and cook, stirring continuously and incorporating the garlic into the bread crumbs so nothing burns, until the bread crumbs are a deep golden brown, about 2 minutes more. Scrape into a small serving bowl and set aside.

Fill a large pot with the broth and add 4 cups water (yes, it seems like a lot of liquid, but it will work out!). Salt it lightly, then bring to a boil; add the pasta and broccoli rabe leaves and adjust the heat to maintain a gentle boil. Cook until the pasta is al dente, a minute or two less than the package instructions, stirring to make sure the pasta isn't sticking together or to the bottom.

While the pasta is cooking, in the skillet you used for the bread crumbs, heat the remaining 2 tablespoons olive oil over medium-high heat until shimmering. Add the remaining garlic, the red pepper flakes, and the anchovies and cook, stirring, so they start to melt in the oil, about 1 minute. Add the broccoli florets and cook until they are bright green and starting to crisp, about 2 minutes. Use a spoon to scoop out some pasta water from the pot, adding a splash or two to the skillet, scraping up anything on the bottom of the pan. Season with salt as needed. Remove from the heat and set aside until the pasta is ready.

When the pasta is done, add the florets to the pot, scraping in any bits, along with the cheese, stirring to combine. Squeeze in half the lemon, then adjust the seasoning as needed with more lemon juice or salt. Ladle into shallow bowls and serve with the bread crumbs, grated cheese, red pepper flakes, for everyone to garnish their soup with.

tip: for the broccoli swap: Use 1 head, and cook half of the florets with the pasta so that it gets super soft and falling apart, and the other half in the pan as directed in the recipe.

lots of mushrooms with farro + provolone
(plus miso, too!)

My favorite part of this recipe is the mushroom metamorphosis—I'm not sure that term can technically be applied to something that isn't growing, but the change is so enormous that it never ceases to amaze me. You'll start with a massive mound of sliced mushrooms in a hot, dry pan, and then you might hear a little squeal or squeak as the steam slowly tries to escape through the narrow gaps between them. They are whittled down until the whole pile collapses, bubbling in its own liquid until that, too, evaporates, leaving you with tiny, shrunken versions of what first was. It's pretty amazing.

Serves 4

Salt

1½ cups farro

3 tablespoons olive oil, divided, plus more for drizzling

2 pounds cremini or mixed mushrooms, stems trimmed and thinly sliced

1 tablespoon white miso paste

2 tablespoons soy sauce

4 ounces Italian provolone (preferably Auricchio), grated

Juice of 1 lime

¼ cup fresh cilantro or parsley, leaves and tender stems, gently torn or chopped

Bring a large pot of lightly salted water to a boil. Add the farro, adjust the heat to maintain a gentle boil, and cook, stirring occasionally, until tender and not overly chewy, about 30 minutes. Drain in a colander in the sink, drizzle with olive oil, and return to the pot.

While the farro is cooking, heat a dry 12-inch cast-iron or other heavy skillet over medium-high heat until very hot, about 2 minutes. Spread the mushrooms in an even layer in the dry pan and lightly season with salt. Cook, undisturbed, for 2 minutes, then stir. Continue to cook and stir every 2 minutes until the mushrooms are shrunken down, golden, and browned, 12 to 14 minutes total. (I know it looks like a massive mound that will never shrink down, but it will, trust me.)

Stir in 2 tablespoons of the olive oil, the miso, and the soy sauce, scraping up anything on the bottom of the pan, and cook until the miso is incorporated, with no clumps remaining, and the soy sauce cooked off, about 1 minute. Remove from the heat and let the mushrooms sit in the residual heat of the pan until the farro is ready.

Return the skillet to medium-low heat and pour in the farro, then add most of the cheese and the remaining 1 tablespoon olive oil. Squeeze in the lime juice and cook until the cheese has mostly melted. Taste and season with salt, then top with the cilantro and remaining cheese, and serve.

some notes: look for a sharp Italian provolone rather than the sliced deli kind. I grate most of the cheese and also cube some so that there are little surprise chunks of cheese throughout. When reheating, add a splash of broth or water to loosen it up, then finish with a drizzle of oil and a squeeze of lime.

it's always winner, winner chicken dinner over here

some basic notes, cooking tips, and marinades

I think the question that I internally cringe at the most (and likely externally, as my face is very expressive) is "What's the best [blank] you've ever been to?" The blank might be the best restaurant I've eaten at in the whole world, the best hotel I've visited, the best restaurant in NYC, and so on. You'd think I'd have some stock answers by now, something to appease the person asking so they move on, but I don't. I usually respond that it's too hard to pick, as it really depends on how I feel and what I'm in the mood for. I'm inevitably met with a blank stare, so I then fumble through a bad answer, leaving them clearly disappointed.

However, when someone asks what I like to cook for friends, I have an answer! It's pretty much always roast chicken because there is something so comforting about the dish—I don't know whether it's the smell, gathering around a gorgeous crispy-skinned bird at the table, or that by surrounding it with some onions and vegetables in the pan, you've already got a built-in juicy, tasty side dish. Throwing another sheet pan of vegetables, like miso-ghee potatoes (page 229) or Brussels sprouts (page 223), into the oven alongside the chicken is a good move for serving a larger crowd.

My friend and food writer Stephanie Burt and I were having a lengthy chat about chicken, as one does, because, as she said, she has "a lot of feelings about chicken and no one wants to listen!" I do, Stephanie—we all do! One of the many things we chatted about was how the quality of the chicken really matters, whether you're cooking a whole bird or chicken parts.

A good-quality chicken will taste delicious with just a little olive oil, salt, and pepper; you don't need much else. But it's also a blank canvas on which you can use so many seasonings and spice combinations, so you won't get sick of it. Kind of like your favorite staple piece of clothing that just goes with everything, can be dressed up or down, and always looks and feels good.

So here are some of my chicken thoughts and feelings.

quality matters

You'll find that there are a good number of chicken recipes in this book, almost to the point where I thought, *Are there too many?* A reason for this is that I discovered the most delicious chicken that I've ever had to date, and it led me into a chicken-cooking frenzy. In New York, I had been lucky to live near so many great butchers, but there wasn't a butcher near me in my new Miami home (without a large delivery fee), so I started looking for frozen chicken, specifically meat from regenerative farms.

I reached out to chef friends, and my friend Katie pointed me toward this particular farm that she said was the best chicken she's ever had. I kid you not, after making my first chicken from that farm, I texted Katie: *You're right! This is the best chicken!* It might sound crazy, but I could tell even by looking at the raw meat that it was going to be good. And the cooked bird was even better than I imagined. I never thought of myself as someone who actually loved chicken, but it was so good that I found myself excited to eat it. (Message me, and I'll tell you more about this chicken and where to find it!)

On that note, I tend to find that chickens from a farmers' market or butcher, one that carefully sources their meat, are smaller and cook faster than their grocery store counterparts, and taste much better. Unfortunately, some chicken is plumped with a liquid solution during processing (which is legal and will be noted on the package), as a way to "marinate" it or to increase the weight so it sells for more. You'll find that these chickens emit liquid when cooked, which is fine, but the cooking time might be a bit longer and your final dish a bit more liquid-y than you expected.

So, this is to say that you should try to buy the best quality and most thoughtfully raised chicken that you can afford because quality really does matter.

lift, pry, and tuck for flavorful meat

It might seem scary the first time you do it, but separating the skin from the meat so you can tuck some seasoning underneath is helpful in not only seasoning the meat itself but also putting a little bit of oil, butter, or ghee under the breast skin helps prevent the meat from drying out (key for Thanksgiving turkeys). Gently lift the skin, then slide a finger (with a short, smooth fingernail) under it and gently "wiggle wiggle" it back and forth, kind of like you're wagging your index finger at someone who has been naughty, to separate the skin from the meat without ripping it. Then add your seasonings, give the skin a little pat to mush everything down, and you're ready to go!

You don't need a lot of fat

A light coating of oil or butter is all you really need; the chicken releases its own fat as it cooks, and, if you add a ton more, it will make all the vegetables the chicken sits on taste oily. I always trim excess fat and skin, the quantity of which depends on the chicken you buy, so it doesn't become overly greasy.

For that crispy, crunchy skin . . .

The secret to crispy skin, whether on a whole bird or some thighs, is simple: Remove moisture from the chicken by using paper towels or a clean dish towel to thoroughly pat the skin dry. You can also air-dry it in the fridge overnight, uncovered, like you might with a turkey. Sticking it under the broiler for 1 to 3 minutes at the end of the cooking time is a cheat method to get some color on the skin, but it's a cheat I use regularly, and there's no shame in that. (Crispy + Crunchy Oregano Chicken is a good place to start, see page 95.)

To fill the cavity or not

Lots of debate on this one for whole birds. I like putting some lemon, salt, or seasonings in the cavity so those flavors seep into the chicken. You can also add some herbs, onions, or other aromatics, but if you find this annoying or don't see the point, then skip it.

No one wants to eat or serve undercooked chicken

If you're someone who worries about serving undercooked chicken—a very valid concern—then the obvious answer is to get a meat thermometer and check that the meat hits 165°F at the thickest part of the thigh. However, unless you get one of the pricier options, these are prone to user error, as you have to be careful where you insert the probe to get an accurate reading, and finding the thickest part of the thigh while you're handling a hot bird, navigating a hot oven, *and* managing dinner guests can be stressful.

Here are some ways to know without one: Grab ahold of the knobby round end of a drumstick and give it a wiggle (I often sing "wiggle wiggle" as I do it); it should feel loose, like you could easily pull it right off without a knife. If it feels a little stiff, like it's clinging to the body, pop the bird back in the oven for 5 to 10 minutes, then check again.

Use a toothpick, a skewer, or the tip of a sharp knife to pierce a thick part of the thigh or lower part of the breast where it meets the thigh. If the juices that run out are clear and look like something you'd want to soak up with bread, then you're good. If they're bloody or reddish, then back into the oven it goes. Now, there are times when chicken will be fully cooked and still a little pink because of proteins that release when cooking, but if it passes every other test, then you're probably fine, which I know is a frustrating answer. If you're unsure, another 5 to 10 minutes in the oven won't hurt you. You can always cover the breast meat with some foil to stop it from drying out and keep cooking.

crispy lemony-yogurt chicken for a crowd

A year-round crowd-pleaser, this dish is best served family-style with a host of other dishes. While the chicken is cooking, I would make the garlicky greens (page 224) on the stovetop, or a no-cook leftover celery + parsley salad (page 210), and/or add a sheet pan of the miso-Parmesan potatoes (page 229) or simple vegetables (page 110) to cook alongside it, so you can serve a delicious family-style meal with chicken, greens, and some sides.

Serves 6

½ cup thick full-fat yogurt, such as Greek yogurt or skyr

2 garlic cloves, grated or minced

2 teaspoons ground cumin

2 teaspoons dried oregano

2 teaspoons honey

¼ teaspoon red pepper flakes

1 lemon, zested, thinly sliced, and seeded

Salt

3½ to 4 pounds bone-in, skin-on chicken parts, such as thighs or drumsticks

1 red onion, cut into ½-inch-thick wedges

2 tablespoons olive oil

¼ cup packed fresh parsley, leaves and tender stems, finely chopped

Heat the oven to 400°F. In a large bowl, combine the yogurt, garlic, cumin, oregano, honey, red pepper flakes, lemon zest, and ½ teaspoon salt. Salt the chicken all over, including under the skin, then add it to the bowl and toss to coat, sneaking some yogurt under the skin, too. Cook immediately or cover and refrigerate until ready to cook, up to 24 hours.

On a sheet pan, combine the onion and lemon slices with the olive oil, lightly seasoning with salt. Spread them over the pan, then add the chicken, skin-side up (it's fine if it covers some of the lemons or onions). Bake until the chicken skin is crispy and the juices run clear when pierced with a fork, 40 to 45 minutes. If there are juices on the sheet pan, spoon some on top of the chicken. Top with the parsley and serve.

spiced + super-lazy roast chicken

There are many ways to roast a chicken, and maybe even more recipes that claim to be the best. I'm going to go out on a limb and dare to say that this might be **the best, laziest chicken recipe out there**. There's no trussing or fussing, turning, snipping, or anything other than some rubbing and tucking (you'll understand when you make it). Even the vegetables are roughly cut into chunks, which even a beginner can comfortably do. My cousin Leyla made me a version of this on my birthday one year, and it was the perfect thing as it's comforting, colorful, and feels so special.

Serves 4

1 (1- to 1½-pound) bag baby yellow potatoes, large ones halved

½ pound carrots, cut into 2-inch chunks

1 red onion, cut into 2-inch-thick wedges

3 or 4 garlic cloves, peeled

3 tablespoons olive oil, divided

Salt

1 (3- to 4-pound) chicken

2 tablespoons ground cumin

1 tablespoon ground turmeric

1 teaspoon dried oregano

1 teaspoon red pepper flakes

Freshly cracked black pepper

1 lemon, cut into wedges

¼ cup fresh dill or parsley, leaves and tender stems, gently torn or chopped

Heat the oven to 400°F. In the bottom of a roasting pan, combine the potatoes, carrots, onion, and garlic and drizzle with 2 tablespoons of the olive oil. Season lightly with salt, toss, and spread out evenly over the pan.

Remove anything in the cavity of the chicken and trim any excess fat and skin, then pat the chicken thoroughly dry. Do it once more after you think it's dry enough. Season all over with salt and set it breast-side up in the center on top of the vegetables.

In a small bowl, mix together the cumin, turmeric, oregano, red pepper flakes, 1 teaspoon salt, and ¼ teaspoon black pepper. Rub the chicken all over with the seasoning mixture, including inside the cavity and under the skin (wear gloves to avoid stained fingers). Tuck the wing tips, if it has them, under the breast area like you're tucking your cold hands into your armpits, and place all but 4 of the lemon wedges inside the cavity. Drizzle the top of the chicken lightly with the remaining 1 tablespoon olive oil.

Roast until the skin is crispy, the thigh juices run clear when pierced with a knife, and the thigh easily wiggles when you lift up the drumstick bone (it should feel like it's about to slip right off), 75 to 90 minutes (larger ones will take 90 minutes). Cover the chicken loosely with foil and let rest for 15 minutes while you set the table and pour the wine.

Top the chicken with the dill and serve with the remaining lemon. Spoon the pan juices on the chicken and vegetables after serving.

note: If you want to use a sheet pan versus a roasting pan (one with higher sides), then add ½ cup of water or broth to the vegetables so that they don't burn.

holiday (or any day) spatchcocked roast chicken, 2 ways

For the past couple of Thanksgivings, I've skipped the turkey in favor of two spatchcocked chickens, each with different rubs. It's not that I don't like turkey—I do—but for some reason, it makes Thanksgiving feel so stressful, and I'm trying to reduce that sort of thing in my life. Chicken is easy, especially if you have your butcher spatchcock it for you, as it cooks quickly and doesn't take up all your oven space. As I'm not a traditionalist, I skip the typical mashed potatoes, cranberry sauce, and stuffing and serve the birds with a variety of roasted vegetables and salads, many of which are in this book, all easy to throw together so that no one, myself included, is stressed out. Here, you'll find one basic recipe with two variations, but you can use any seasonings that you like.

Serves 4

1 (3- to 4-pound) chicken, spatchcocked (see note, please!)

Olive oil

Salt

1 head garlic or individual, unpeeled cloves (optional)

for spiced chicken:
2 to 3 tablespoons za'atar, plus more for garnish

Or (if za'atar is hard to find)

2 teaspoons dried oregano

1 teaspoon ground cumin

1 teaspoon pimétón (smoked paprika)

½ teaspoon red pepper flakes

for miso-ghee chicken:
1 tablespoon ghee or unsalted butter, at room temperature

2 teaspoons white miso paste

Heat the oven to 400°F with a rack 6 inches from the broiler heat source. Pat the chicken dry all over. Like really, really dry. Drizzle all over with olive oil, then season with salt (generously for a spiced chicken or lightly for a miso bird).

Lay the chicken breast-side up in the center of a sheet pan and coat the top with the za'atar, or stir together the miso and ghee and spread it over the bird. Use your forefinger (with a short fingernail) to pry open the space between the skin and the breast meat and add the oil/spices or miso and ghee under there, using your finger to spread it around as best you can. Cut the top off the garlic at the knot, if using, then drizzle generously with oil and sprinkle with salt or generously oil the unpeeled cloves. Wrap the garlic in foil and set in the corner of the sheet pan.

Roast the chicken until the juices run clear when pierced with a fork and the skin is browned and crispy, about 45 minutes. Turn the broiler on, if you need a bit of extra crisp, and place the chicken under the broiler until the skin is browned, 1 to 3 minutes, depending on the strength of your broiler. Serve with the roasted garlic, squeezing out the cloves to eat with bread or slather on the meat.

how to spatchcock: Use sharp shears to cut along both sides of the backbone. Flip the chicken, then use both your hands to firmly press down on the breastbone until you hear a crack and the bird flattens. Adjust the legs so it looks like its knees are knocking in (fine if you forget this step! I know we did in the photo—mistakes happen, but it still tasted great!)

185

gingery chicken with tomatoes + onions + potatoes

When I made this dish for a friend, he said, "This looks so cozy and pretty, I would have thought it was hard to make, if you didn't tell me otherwise." I probably shouldn't have told him that it's fairly low-effort. Kind of like when someone says, "I love your dress!" and without fail I share that I got it on the cheap. Just take the compliment, Yaz!

Anyway, this dish has a cooking method similar in theory to a tagine, where food is slowly cooked, first covered, so that everything becomes steamy and tender, then uncovered, so that the ingredients brown a little. Serve it with bread or with rice to soak up the flavorful juices.

Serves 4

1 (2-inch) piece fresh ginger: grate half to get 1 teaspoon ginger, then thinly slice the remaining half (you'll have 4 or 5 slices)

2 teaspoons ground turmeric

1 tablespoon ground oregano

1 tablespoon ground cumin

1 teaspoon red pepper flakes

Freshly ground black pepper

¼ cup olive oil, divided

2½ pounds bone-in, skin-on chicken parts, such as thighs, drumsticks, or legs

Salt

1 pint grape tomatoes or cherry tomatoes

1 pound baby Yukon Gold potatoes, halved

1 small red onion, sliced into ½-inch-thick wedges

½ cup low-sodium chicken or vegetable broth or water

Juice of 1 large lemon (about 3 tablespoons)

¼ cup fresh cilantro or parsley, leaves and tender stems, or mint leaves, gently torn or chopped

Crusty bread or cooked rice, for serving

Heat the oven to 400°F. In a medium bowl, mix together the grated ginger, turmeric, oregano, cumin, red pepper flakes, a few hefty grinds of black pepper, and 3 tablespoons of the olive oil. Pat the chicken dry and season all over with salt. Add the chicken to the spice rub, turning to coat it all over and sneaking some under the skin (wear gloves if you don't want turmeric-stained fingers).

In a 9 by 13-inch baking dish, combine the tomatoes, potatoes, red onion, and ginger slices and season with salt, black pepper, and the remaining 1 tablespoon olive oil (the dish will look crowded, and that's okay). Pour in the broth and lemon juice and mix the ingredients to combine. Place the chicken pieces on top, skin-side up. Cover with foil and bake for 1 hour. Remove the foil, spoon some of the juices over the chicken, and bake, uncovered, for 30 minutes more, until the meat is falling-off-the-bone tender. Fish out the ginger slices, if you can find them, or warn guests that they look deceptively like potatoes when bathed in this golden broth. Top with the cilantro and serve with crusty bread for dipping or rice.

easy sunday meat sauce

This recipe started out as an untraditional Bolognese full of mushrooms, and it failed spectacularly. The note to myself was, "This was bad." Instead, here is a simple and hearty big bowl of steamy, meat-rich sauce with a few warming spices (can't escape the cumin!) to let simmer while you sip some wine.

Serves 4 to 6

2 tablespoons olive oil

1 yellow onion, diced

1 small to medium carrot, cut into thin rounds or diced

Salt

1 pound 80/20 ground beef

2 teaspoons ground turmeric

1 teaspoon ground cumin

Freshly ground black pepper

½ teaspoon red pepper flakes

2 tablespoons tomato paste

½ cup good-quality red wine, preferably what you're drinking

2 (28-ounce) cans crushed tomatoes

Parmesan rind (optional)

1 pound long pasta, such as spaghetti, bucatini, or tagliatelle

Grated Parmesan, for garnish

¼ cup fresh basil, leaves and tender stems, gently torn

Heat the olive oil in a 12-inch skillet or Dutch oven over medium-high heat until shimmering. Add the onion and carrot, season lightly with salt, and cook, stirring occasionally, until the onion and carrot soften, 6 to 8 minutes. Stir in the ground beef, turmeric, cumin, a few grinds of black pepper, and the red pepper flakes. Season lightly with salt and cook, breaking up the beef into small, crumbly pieces, until the meat is browned all over with some crispy spots and no pink remains, 8 to 10 minutes.

Move the meat mixture to the sides of the pot and add the tomato paste to the center, stirring so it gets contact with the pan then mixing it all together, about 1 minute. Stir in the wine and cook until it has just about disappeared, about 30 seconds. Pour in the crushed tomatoes, then fill both cans a quarter of the way with water, swirl them to get anything clinging to the sides, and pour into the pot. Add the Parmesan rind, if using. Raise the heat to bring the liquid to a gentle boil, then reduce the heat to maintain a gentle simmer with small bubbles breaking across the surface and cook until it thickens and the sauce becomes rich and flavorful, 40 minutes or up to 2 hours. If the sauce looks too thick or dry at any point, add ¼ cup water to loosen it. This sauce can simmer and hold up, so no need to rush it.

About 15 minutes before you're ready to eat, bring a large pot of well-salted water to a boil. Add the pasta and cook until just shy of al dente, 2 to 3 minutes less than the package instructions. Use tongs to transfer the pasta to the pot with the sauce, bringing along some water clinging to the noodles. Toss to coat. Add another spoonful or two as needed if it doesn't look saucy. Cook, allowing the noodles to soak up some of the sauce, 2 to 3 minutes more. Season with salt as needed and finish with the cheese and basil.

meatballs + tomato sauce!!

I used to hold the strong opinion that meatballs had to be made of three meats: pork, beef, and veal. Single-meat meatballs just didn't cut it—the flavor was flat and one-dimensional. I've softened with time, and now the idea of buying three different kinds of meats feels oddly exhausting, so beef it is. You'll notice some oddities, as I stray from traditional Italian meatballs (please don't yell at me, internet!). The cumin is a wildly untraditional spin—but I truly feel it makes everything better. There is also no egg in this recipe, because I found that the meat held together well enough without it.

If you're having guests, you can shape the meatballs, place them in the fridge, and let the sauce simmer until the doorbell rings, then pop the meatballs in the oven and add them to the sauce when ready to serve.

Makes 16 to 18 meatballs

for the meatballs

3 tablespoons olive oil, divided

2 garlic cloves, grated or minced

½ to 1 teaspoon red pepper flakes, depending on your heat preference

2 teaspoons ground cumin

Salt

¼ cup packed fresh flat-leaf parsley or basil, finely chopped

½ cup ricotta cheese, strained, if necessary

¼ cup grated Parmesan

¼ cup panko bread crumbs

1 pound 80/20 ground beef

the meatballs

Heat the oven to 400°F. Use 1 tablespoon oil to coat a sheet pan. In a large bowl, combine the garlic, red pepper flakes, cumin, 1 teaspoon salt, the parsley, ricotta, Parmesan, bread crumbs, and remaining olive oil. Gently mix in the ground beef until there's some green specks peppering the entire mixture. Wet or oil your palms, then shape the meat into balls, each slightly larger than a golf ball, placing them on the prepared sheet pan as you go. You should have 16 to 18 meatballs. Bake for 15 minutes.

for the sauce

2 tablespoons olive oil

1 small red onion, thinly sliced

Salt

2 garlic cloves, grated or minced

¼ to ½ teaspoon red pepper flakes, depending on your heat preference

2 tablespoons tomato paste

½ cup red wine, preferably what you're drinking

2 (28-ounce) cans crushed tomatoes

Parmesan rind (optional)

¼ cup grated Parmesan, or more as needed

¼ cup fresh basil, leaves and tender stems, gently torn or chopped (optional)

Bread or cooked polenta (see page 163), for serving

the sauce

Heat the olive oil in a Dutch oven or large braising dish over medium-high heat until shimmering. Add the onion, season with salt, and cook, stirring occasionally, until it starts to soften, about 5 minutes. Add the garlic and red pepper flakes and cook until fragrant, about 30 seconds. Make a space in the center, then add the tomato paste, stirring it into the rest of the dish until it's a fiery red color, about 2 minutes more. Add the wine and cook until it mostly bubbles away and there's little liquid remaining, 1 to 2 minutes.

Pour in the canned tomatoes and add the Parmesan rind, if using, then raise the heat to bring it to a gentle boil. Adjust the heat to maintain a simmer, with small bubbles forming across the pan rather than wildly erupting (I don't know why that scares me a bit, but it does). Cook, stirring occasionally, tasting, and adding salt as needed, until it thickens and the canned taste has cooked off, at least 30 minutes or up to 45, if you have the time. Nestle the meatballs in the sauce and cook over low heat for 2 to 3 minutes, letting them warm up. Top with a generous dousing of Parmesan and basil, if using, and serve with bread.

last thought: Use leftover ricotta as an appetizer dip by making a well in the center and filling it with good olive oil, some red pepper flakes, and a nice flaky salt.

easy baked lasagna with broccolini

My friend Tom requested that I put a lasagna recipe in this book, something I'd avoided in my previous books because, by nature, it's a time-consuming dish (aka one I rarely work up the energy to make, despite its high comfort level). So I've tried to use some tasty shortcuts to keep it as simple as possible, but it's still a recipe to make when you've got some energy and a hearty appetite, and are looking forward to feeding a crowd. It's also sprinkled with my true love, Broccolini (or broccoli!), so the sauce is both meat and vegetable filled (the pieces end up being so tiny that you—or vegetable-averse eaters—might not notice them).

There are more steps here than in most recipes in the book, so I would read through it once carefully, and go slowly, as each step is simple, probably things you've done before, it just seems like a lot all together. I have faith in you! (You can always sip on a glass of wine if you're feel overwhelmed at any point.)

Serves 6 to 8

2 tablespoons olive oil

1 medium yellow onion, diced

Salt

1 pound Italian-style sausage (pork, turkey, or chicken), removed from its casings

2 bunches Broccolini, ends trimmed and finely chopped, or 1 small head broccoli, florets and tender stalks finely chopped

2 or 3 garlic cloves, grated or minced

½ to 1 teaspoon red pepper flakes, depending on your heat preference

1 cup packed fresh flat-leaf parsley, finely chopped

8 ounces lasagna noodles (not the no-boil ones)

2 tablespoons tomato paste

¼ cup red wine

2 (28-ounce) cans crushed tomatoes

Heat the oven to 400°F. Heat the olive oil in your biggest deep skillet or Dutch oven over medium-high heat until shimmering. Add the onion, season lightly with salt, and cook, stirring occasionally, until just starting to soften, about 5 minutes. Add the sausage, Broccolini, garlic, red pepper flakes, three-quarters of the parsley and season lightly with salt. It will look like a messy, grassy pile, and that's great! Stir it all together, then cook, slowly breaking up the meat into a combination of small chunks and crumbly bits as you stir every minute or two, until no raw pink remains, 7 to 9 minutes.

While the sausage is cooking, fill a large shallow bowl or deep pan with very hot tap water, mix in some salt, and layer the noodles in, making sure to separate and shift them around so nothing is sticking together. Leave the noodles fully covered with water until the sauce is ready.

Push the ingredients in the skillet to the edges, making a center stage, add the tomato paste, stir, and leave it to cook in that little circle until it's a fiery red color, about 2 minutes. Stir to combine the paste with the other ingredients. Then pour in the wine and cook until most of the bubbling liquid in the bottom of the pan has disappeared, about 2 minutes. (Also a good time to break up any large sausage chunks you missed.) Pour in the crushed tomatoes

1 cup fresh ricotta, strained, if necessary

1¼ cups grated Pecorino Romano or Parmesan

1 (8- to 10-ounce) ball mozzarella, torn into small, bite-size pieces

¼ cup packed fresh basil, leaves and tender stems, gently torn or chopped (optional)

and adjust the heat to maintain a gentle simmer. Cook until the canned taste cooks off and the sauce has thickened, about 20 minutes. Taste your sauce and make sure it has enough heat, salt, and so on, keeping in mind that the cheese will add a fair amount of salt, too.

While the sauce simmers, in a medium bowl, mix together the ricotta, 1 cup of the pecorino, and the remaining parsley until combined.

Drain the noodles as best you can. In the bottom of a 9 by 13-inch baking dish, spread a layer of sauce—this is for the noodles to soak up, so be generous. Layer half the noodles on top of the sauce, then add a light layer of the cheese mixture and top it with one-third of the mozzarella, remembering that it will spread out as it melts, so it shouldn't fully cover the sauce. Add another layer of sauce, then add the remaining noodles, breaking up any pieces as needed to cover the sauce layer fully. Top with another layer of the cheese mixture, another mozzarella layer, and more sauce. Completely cover the top with the remaining mozzarella and pecorino; the sauce on top should be an off-white color.

Place the baking dish on a sheet pan in case anything spills over (this also makes it easier to move in and out of the oven) and bake until the top is bubbling and the lasagna at the edges of the pan is browned and crisp, 30 minutes. Let cool for 10 minutes, then sprinkle with the basil, if using, and serve.

noodle note: Also know that if any noodles rip while you're moving them, it's all good—just tuck those pieces in the awkward and imperfect corners that need some covering.

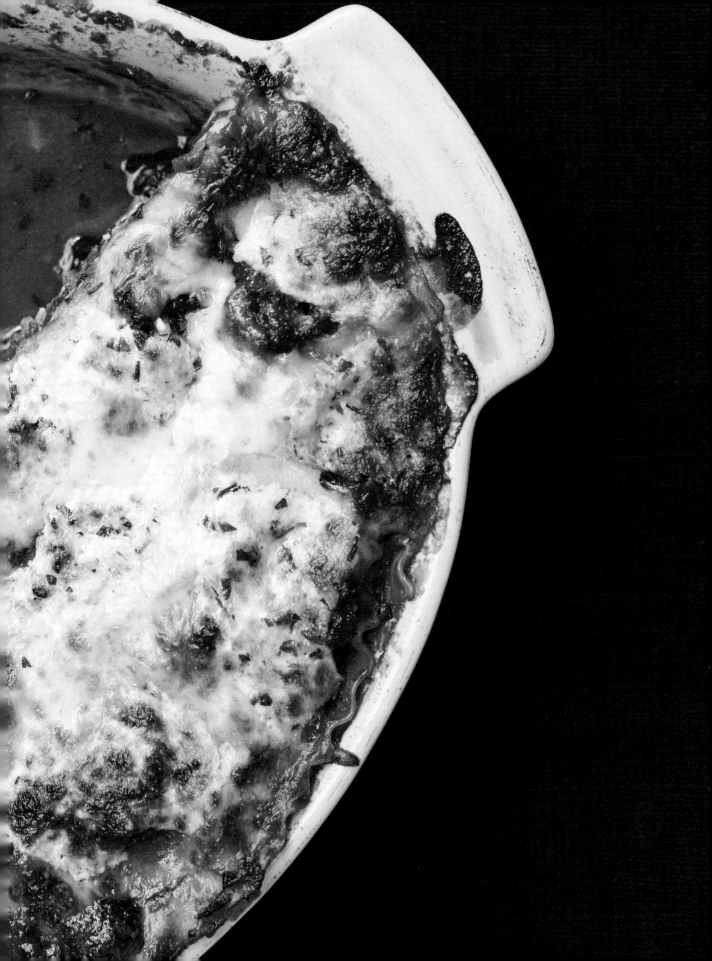

big bowl salads + medium sides

I remember reading in the *New Yorker,* many, many years ago, that Michelin inspectors didn't order salad at restaurants, which I found bizarre. That's one of the two criteria I judge a restaurant on: How are their salads, and how are their bathrooms? Both utterly important, for different reasons. For each, it's the amount of detail, care, and thought that went into creating them. If you're putting thought and care into the smallest parts of your operation, then it's likely everything has gotten that amount of attention. For a salad, are the greens gorgeous? Is the dressing a simple but evocative one that makes you want to order the salad and feel glad you did when it arrives? Via Carota's massive mound of a salad comes to mind.

This is all to say that I don't ignore salads on menus—I love them, and I hope you'll love the variety in this section, too, from simple everyday green salads that can be served alongside any dish in this book to a heartier three-herb farro salad that can be a meal of its own with a little something on top (I give you more specifics in the recipe, don't worry). These all serve four people as a side dish, or they can be eaten on their own with simply cooked chicken thighs or salmon or another side dish, if you want something lighter for one or two people. Speaking of sides, you'll also find a bunch of "composed vegetable sides," or perhaps better titled, "more interesting vegetable sides" versus the simple options in The Mighty Vegetable section (page 108) that you can use to bulk up a meal, or even make a bunch of them for a mostly vegetable spread. All serve four people as an appetizer or side dish.

how to use these recipes: You can eat these solo with some added protein on top or pair them with another dish or two from this section or any other chapters.

asparagus salad with pecorino + herbs

Recipes will often cue you to soak shallots or onions in water, which takes away that bite that can give you terrible dragon's breath. Here, you'll place them in the dressing to soften, and then pour it all on top of the asparagus, so you can skip that soaking step. You can also put this on top of a bed of greens or grains and mix in other vegetables like thinly sliced radishes or chunks of avocado.

2 tablespoons sherry vinegar or red wine vinegar

1 tablespoon Dijon mustard

1 teaspoon white miso paste

¼ cup extra-virgin olive oil

1 small shallot, or ¼ red onion, diced

¼ cup pumpkin seeds, shelled pistachios, or pine nuts

1 bunch asparagus, ends trimmed

2 tablespoons packed fresh dill or mint, or ¼ cup packed fresh basil or parsley, leaves and tender stems, gently torn

¼ cup shaved Pecorino Romano or grated Parmesan

Flaky sea salt and freshly cracked black pepper

In the bottom of a serving bowl, mix together the vinegar, mustard, miso, and olive oil until it has a creamy, cohesive texture. Toss the shallot in the dressing and let sit.

Meanwhile, add the nuts to a dry skillet over medium heat, stirring occasionally, until they just start to brown and pop, 3 to 5 minutes. Remove from the heat and let the residual heat of the pan finish toasting them. Peel the asparagus into ribbons with a vegetable peeler, discarding the fibrous outermost layer.

Mix the asparagus into the dressing and top with the toasted nuts, dill, and cheese. Season with flaky salt and a few grinds of pepper, and serve.

cucumber salad with mint, dill, feta + lime dressing

I read once in a Maine supermarket produce section that the inside of a cucumber is at least 10 degrees cooler than the outside, likely where the saying "cool as a cucumber" came from, and that makes perfect sense. This cooling salad does just that; plus, the tangle of fresh herbs, feta and spices, brightened with fresh lime juice makes it refreshing, simple, and crunchy. Pair it with something heartier like roast chicken, salmon, pasta, or bulk it up by adding a handful of chickpeas or croutons.

¼ teaspoon ground cumin

¼ teaspoon red pepper flakes, plus more as needed

½ teaspoon Dijon mustard

Juice of 2 limes

2 tablespoons olive oil

Salt

¼ cup packed fresh dill, leaves and tender stems, finely chopped

¼ cup packed fresh mint leaves, finely chopped, plus some leaves left whole for garnish

6 to 7 Persian cucumbers, or ½ English cucumber

¼ cup crumbled feta, preferably Bulgarian

In a large bowl, whisk together the cumin, red pepper flakes, mustard, lime juice, and olive oil until smooth. Season to taste with salt. Mix in two-thirds of the dill and two-thirds of the mint (sorry if this makes you feel like you're doing math—eyeballing it is great!).

Halve the cucumbers lengthwise. Lay them skin-side down on your cutting board and firmly press down on them with the heel of your palm or the flat side of your chef's knife to smash them. Cut into bite-size pieces.

Add the cucumbers and two-thirds of the feta to the bowl with the dressing and toss to coat. Let sit for 5 minutes, then toss again. Sprinkle the remaining feta and herbs on top. Season as needed with salt and more red pepper flakes.

miso-charred corn with broccolini panzanella

Someone once asked me, "Have you ever had a recipe that you just couldn't get published in the world?" And no, not really, but if there were one, it would be a variation of this with miso croutons that no one seemed interested in—and I don't understand why. It's one of my favorites, full of crunchy bites: charred corn, Broccolini, and (regular) croutons. My neighbor took some of the extras of this and later said to me, "What was that dressing? I loved it!" So I hope you enjoy this fun big bowl salad to serve for friends or as part of a spread, though tossing the croutons with some miso butter or ghee straight out of the oven would be delightful.

2 teaspoons white miso paste

2 tablespoons grated Parmesan

1 tablespoon sherry vinegar or red wine vinegar, plus a splash or more (about 1 teaspoon) for the pan

¼ cup olive oil, divided

2 cups croutons (see page 205)

2 ears corn, kernels removed (about 2 cups)

Salt

1 bunch Broccolini, ends trimmed, or 1 small head broccoli, florets cut into bite-size pieces (2 to 3 cups)

Pinch of red pepper flakes

3 scallions, light green and white parts, thinly sliced

3 cups packed baby arugula, plus more if needed

In a large serving bowl, mash together the miso, Parmesan, vinegar, and 2 tablespoons of the olive oil and combine as best you can. Add the croutons and toss to coat; set aside.

Heat the remaining 2 tablespoons oil in a 12-inch cast-iron skillet over medium-high heat until shimmering. Add the corn kernels, season lightly with salt, and cook, undisturbed, until the bottoms start crackling, about 2 minutes. Stir, then cook, undisturbed, for another 2 minutes. Add the Broccolini pieces and cook, stirring occasionally, until the corn and Broccolini are charred in spots, 8 to 10 minutes more. Add the red pepper flakes, scallions, and a splash of vinegar. Cook, stirring and scraping up anything on the bottom of the pan, until the liquid bubbles off, about 30 seconds.

Scrape the vegetable mixture into the serving bowl and toss with the dressing. Season as needed with more vinegar or salt. If you're serving right away, add the arugula; otherwise, add the arugula just before serving. If you think the salad is too soaked with dressing, add a bit more arugula and toss to combine.

croutons, two ways

I love a good crouton: You use up some stale bread, random odds and ends you didn't get to eat, and you get something crunchy and tasty that loves a good soak in a dressing or sauce. While oven croutons are a good option because they're hands-off and you can make a larger batch, I also love the stovetop method because it's quick, no heating of the oven necessary, and you can make just what you need for right now, which is also great when you have only a little bread to work with.

to make

2 cups bite-size pieces = about ¼ classic French baguette or 3 thick slices country-style bread

3 cups = about ½ classic French baguette or 4 thick slices country-style bread

When tearing or cutting the bread into bite-size pieces, asking yourself, *Could I comfortably take a bite of this if it were on my plate?*

stovetop croutons
Stale or fresh bread, however much will comfortably fit in a skillet

Olive oil

Salt

Heat a dry Dutch oven or a 12-inch cast-iron or other heavy skillet over medium-high heat until hot, about 2 minutes. Add the bread, let it toast for 1 minute, then drizzle with 2 tablespoons of olive oil or until most pieces have a bit of oil on them. Season with a full moon of salt and stir to coat. Cook, turning the pieces over as needed, until crunchy and golden brown, 6 to 8 minutes more. Let cool off the heat until you can bite into them without burning yourself, then enjoy.

oven (or toaster oven) croutons

½ baguette, or 4 thick slices country-style bread

Olive oil

Salt

Heat the oven (or toaster oven) to 400°F. Tear the bread into bite-size pieces, toss on a sheet pan with 2 to 3 waves olive oil until lightly coated, and season with 1 wave of salt. Bake for 8 to 10 minutes, until golden and browned in spots. Set aside to cool, remembering that they will darken slightly as they cool.

everyday big bowl salad
(with a vinegary dressing)

This is a salad that I've been making since my early twenties, when I was so excited to fill up this large white salad bowl that I loved, curl up on the couch, and eat it entirely by myself. The variations are endless, but the core remains the same. Add as many extras as you want or keep it simple and plain with just lettuce, dressing, and an avocado—something I do on particularly hot days or if I feel like I've been eating a lot more than usual and want something light and easy. Switch up the vinegars or acid depending on your mood, preference, or availability. Red wine vinegar, sherry vinegar, or lemon juice would all work wonderfully.

2 teaspoons Dijon mustard

¼ cup apple cider vinegar

¼ cup olive oil

Salt and freshly cracked black pepper

Pinch of red pepper flakes (optional)

1 large head crunchy lettuce (9 to 10 ounces), like a romaine heart, butter, or Boston, gently torn or chopped

1 (13.5-ounce) can chickpeas or white beans, such as cannellini or navy, drained and rinsed

1 ripe Hass avocado, cubed

¼ cup packed fresh basil or cilantro, gently torn or chopped

¼ cup crumbled feta or grated Parmesan

2 tablespoons nuts or seeds, such as pumpkin seeds, sunflower seeds, or shelled pistachios, lightly toasted (see page 201)

In the bottom of your big bowl, whisk together the mustard, vinegar, and olive oil until smooth. Season to taste with salt, a couple grinds of black pepper, and some red pepper flakes, if using. Add the lettuce, chickpeas, avocado, and basil and toss to coat in the dressing. Garnish with the cheese and nuts.

note: If you're making this for one person, halve the quantities. You could also halve the beans when making it for two, if you're not a big bean person, then use the remaining beans in another salad or soup in the next couple of days, if you remember.

zucchini salad with chickpeas, cheese + a mustardy dressing

A punchy dressing that helps spruce up the otherwise blank-slate (aka kind of bland) squash with 15 to 30 minutes of marinating, making this is a lovely salad that works well for lunch on hot summer days when you don't want to turn on the stove or oven. It also works wonderfully as a side dish to bring to picnics or outdoor gatherings, as it gets better the longer it sits in the dressing. Zucchini skin is very thin, so it's fine to eat, but you can trim off any damaged spots.

¼ to ½ teaspoon red pepper flakes, depending on your heat preference

½ teaspoon ground cumin

1 teaspoon Dijon mustard

Zest and juice of 1 large lemon (about 1 tablespoon zest and 3 tablespoons juice)

2 tablespoons extra-virgin olive oil

Salt

2 large zucchini or summer squash

1 (15-ounce) can chickpeas, drained and rinsed

½ cup crumbled soft white cheese, such as feta, Oaxaca cheese, or queso fresco

¼ cup fresh basil, mint, or cilantro leaves, gently chopped or torn

Freshly cracked black pepper

2 to 3 cups packed baby spinach

In a large serving bowl, whisk together the red pepper flakes, cumin, mustard, lemon zest, lemon juice, and olive oil until smooth. Season lightly with salt, taste, and adjust again as needed.

Halve the zucchini lengthwise, then scoop out the seeds with a spoon. Use a vegetable peeler to peel the zucchini into ribbons. When you can't peel any more ribbons, coarsely chop the odd middle and end parts into small pieces that can easily be picked up with a fork (this will give the salad some fun texture). Add the zucchini and the chickpeas to the bowl with the dressing. Toss well to combine. Set aside on the counter for 15 to 30 minutes to let the zucchini soak up the dressing.

Mix in the cheese and basil, and season to taste with salt or black pepper as needed. Add the spinach to the bowl (or add a handful each to individual servings if you're serving the salad later) and toss to soak up any lingering liquid.

three-herb farro salad

This salad lives somewhere between a main course and a side dish, as it's too substantial to be relegated to merely a side salad but not ready to fly fully solo without a buddy. It's the perfect thing to add to a dinner or spread when you are worried if there will be enough food. Whether that means eating it with Ginger-Soy Salmon (page 71) or Crispy Lemony-Yogurt Chicken for a Crowd (page 183), or simply searing some Halloumi as a swap for the feta, it needs something, someone (don't we all?!).

Salt

1 cup farro, rinsed

2 tablespoons apple cider vinegar

2 teaspoons Dijon mustard

¼ teaspoon ground cumin

¼ teaspoon red pepper flakes

2 tablespoons olive oil, plus more for the farro

Leaves and tender stems from 1 bunch cilantro, finely chopped (about 1 packed cup; reserve some whole leaves for garnish)

Leaves and tender stems from 1 small bunch parsley, finely chopped (about 1 packed cup; reserve some whole leaves for garnish)

½ cup packed fresh dill, finely chopped (reserve some whole leaves for garnish)

2 scallions, thinly sliced

4 Persian cucumbers, thinly sliced, or ½ English cucumber, halved and thinly sliced

1 (15-ounce) can chickpeas, drained and rinsed

Juice of 1 lime

½ cup crumbled feta, preferably Bulgarian

Bring a large pot of well-salted water to a boil. Add the farro, adjust the heat to maintain a gentle boil (no scary bubbles), and cook until tender and no longer chewy, about 30 minutes.

Meanwhile, in a large serving bowl, mix together the vinegar, mustard, cumin, red pepper flakes, and olive oil until smooth. Add the cilantro, parsley, dill, scallions, cucumbers, and chickpeas. Season with salt and toss to combine. Let sit until the farro is ready.

Drain the farro, shake off excess water, and drizzle lightly with olive oil and the lime juice, then toss to combine. Let cool for 5 minutes, then, while the farro is still warm (but not too hot), add it to the bowl with the dressing. Season as needed with salt, then top with the reserved whole herb leaves and the feta, and serve.

to chop herbs quickly: For soft herbs like dill, parsley, and cilantro, you can leave the tender stems on, so no need to pick the leaves from the stem unless you use mint. Chop off the thick stalks, then bunch together and hold the tip of your chef's knife with one hand while you move the knife across the bunch. Bunch again and repeat until finely chopped. (I find this fun and satisfying, and I hope you do, too!)

leftover celery + parsley salad
(with lemon-mustard dressing + parmesan)

While testing some recipes for a friend, one of which was a chicken soup that called for one stalk of celery, I felt annoyed (not at her, but at the recipe, if you can separate the two). That one stalk aside, what was I supposed to do with the remaining stalks in the bunch? I find this happens often, and, while I want to say I cleverly use them, I don't; they often wilt and soften in my fridge, until they are limp and sad looking, and then I feel guilty and throw them out. So here is the salad to make when you've only used a stalk or two of your celery and don't feel like munching on the rest.

It's crunchy and full of greenery, and makes a nice addition to cooked meats, especially in the summer, but it could also add a little sunshine during gloomy winter months. This salad would also do well finished with some fresh mint, dill, or basil, depending on the time of year you make it and what you have in the house.

Serves 4

¼ teaspoon red pepper flakes

1 teaspoon white miso paste

1 tablespoon Dijon mustard

Juice of 1 large lemon (about 3 tablespoons)

2 tablespoons olive oil

1 bunch celery, minus 1 or 2 stalks is fine, trimmed and thinly sliced

1 bunch parsley, leaves and tender stems chopped a couple of times or torn, so they are still leafy (about 1 cup packed)

¼ cup grated Parmesan

Salt and freshly cracked black pepper

In a large serving bowl, combine the red pepper flakes, miso, mustard, lemon juice, and olive oil until smooth, using a fork to break the miso apart if it's clumpy (a few small clumps are fine). Add the celery, parsley (it will look like a lot to add, but it will work out, I promise!), and most of the Parmesan, reserving a little for garnish, then toss to coat with the dressing.

Let sit in the fridge, uncovered, for 15 minutes. Season to taste with salt, a few grinds of black pepper, and the remaining Parmesan.

quick thoughts for some add-ins: chickpeas or white beans; lightly toasted pumpkin seeds or pine nuts

blistered olive + asparagus salad with feta + turmeric-stained onions

While staying at my friend Sally's flat in London in early May one year, I got to enjoy the first signs of English asparagus, so I immediately bought some, along with feta, garlic-lemon olives, and some stunning eggs, at Portobello Market. This version skips the eggs (though they would be great for a solo/duo meal), and adds turmeric-stained onions. I love the way the lime in the onions plays off the vinegar in the asparagus, but you could also skip the vinegar and use lime juice throughout. If you have time, then make the onions at least 15 minutes before, or even the day before, waiting to add the herbs until serving so they stay fresh.

Juice of 2 limes

Freshly cracked black pepper

¼ teaspoon ground turmeric

3 tablespoons olive oil, divided

Salt

1 small red onion, thinly sliced

¼ cup packed fresh cilantro or parsley, leaves and tender stems, gently torn or chopped

1 bunch asparagus, ends trimmed

1 cup green olives, pitted, smashed (see page 67), and chopped once or twice

¼ teaspoon red pepper flakes

2 tablespoons sherry vinegar, red wine vinegar, or apple cider vinegar

½ cup crumbled feta, preferably Bulgarian

In a small bowl, whisk together the lime juice, a few grinds of black pepper, the turmeric, and 1 tablespoon of the olive oil. Season lightly with salt. Mix in the onion and cilantro. Set aside.

Heat the remaining 2 tablespoons oil in a 12-inch skillet over medium-high heat until shimmering. Add the asparagus, season lightly with salt, and cook, undisturbed, for 2 minutes. Stir, then add the olives and red pepper flakes. Cook, stirring occasionally, until the asparagus is blistered in spots and crisp-tender, 6 to 8 minutes more, depending on the thickness of the stalks. Add the vinegar and cook, stirring, until the liquid cooks off, about 1 minute more. Transfer to a serving plate.

Top with the feta and a handful of the turmeric onions, serving the rest on the side. Finish with a few grinds of black pepper.

lentil salad with celery + an acidic dressing

I often cook a big batch of lentils at the start of the week so I can make this salad on repeat for lunch as it's acidic, crunchy, and both filling and light. For dinner, this is another salad that is best served with a buddy. It can be simply cooked white fish or Halloumi, or maybe you add it to a green salad for bulk and protein. Roast chicken is also a friend. These lentils stay firm while cooking and still have a bit of bite to them.

Serves 4

Salt

1 cup French green Le Puy or brown Spanish lentils (soak for at least an hour or overnight or don't, up to you and your tummy!)

2 tablespoons sherry vinegar, red wine vinegar, or apple cider vinegar

2 teaspoons Dijon mustard

Red pepper flakes

2 tablespoons olive oil

1 shallot, or ½ small red onion, minced

2 celery stalks, thinly sliced (use the rest in leftover celery salad, page 210)

2 tablespoons grated Parmesan

½ cup packed fresh parsley, leaves and tender stems, gently torn or chopped

Freshly cracked black pepper

Bring a large pot of well-salted water to a boil. Add the lentils, adjust the heat to maintain a simmer, and cook until the lentils are tender and no longer chewy, 25 to 30 minutes. Skim any frothy bits off the top. Drain, shaking off excess water.

While the lentils are cooking, in a large serving bowl, whisk together the vinegar, mustard, red pepper flakes (use anywhere from a pinch up to ¼ teaspoon, depending on your heat preference), and the olive oil and whisk until smooth. Add the shallot, celery, and a pinch or two of salt, toss to coat, and let sit until the lentils are ready.

Add the drained lentils to the dressing and toss to combine. Mix in the Parmesan, then let the flavors blend for 10 minutes or longer. Mix in the parsley and season as needed with salt and black pepper before serving.

charred brussels sprout salad with miso-yogurt dressing, two ways

I first made the raw version of this salad for a Thanksgiving spread, and it was the perfect accompaniment, as it's light and flavorful but not overpowering. The half-cooked version is great when you're serving it for a less intense spread than a Thanksgiving meal, as the two textures provide a nice variety so it doesn't feel like it's getting boring. The cutting of the sprouts is annoying, but I tend to put on a mindless show (or even *Love Actually*, if it's anywhere remotely near Christmastime) and slice away—I've even moved the entire cutting operation into the living room. I'm not saying that these are habits you should adopt, but this is what I do when no one is watching, and it makes the prep work less annoying (you can also buy pre-cut sprouts to save yourself time).

You can make the dressing the day before, as the longer this salad sits, the better it tastes. Bring it to room temperature before serving, squeeze half a lemon over it, drizzle with olive oil, mix, and serve.

In a large serving bowl, mix the yogurt, miso, lemon juice, and olive oil until smooth. Taste and season with salt as needed. Mix in the Brussels sprouts, coating them with the dressing. Cover and let sit in the fridge overnight or for at least 30 minutes.

brussels sprouts in their birthday suits (raw version)

½ cup thick full-fat yogurt, such as Greek yogurt or skyr

1 tablespoon white miso paste

Juice of 1 lemon (about 3 tablespoons)

2 tablespoons olive oil

Salt

2 pounds Brussels sprouts, trimmed and thinly sliced

Heat 2 tablespoons of the olive oil in a 12-inch cast-iron or other heavy skillet over medium-high heat until shimmering. Add half the Brussels sprouts, season lightly with salt, then let sit for 2 minutes, undisturbed. Stir again, then continue cooking and stirring at 2-minute intervals until lightly colored in spots and wilted, about 6 minutes total. Let cool slightly off the heat.

Meanwhile, in a large serving bowl, combine the yogurt, miso, lemon juice, and remaining 2 tablespoons olive oil until smooth. Taste and season with salt. Mix in the raw sprouts, then, once the cooked ones are lightly cooled, mix them in as well. Cover and let sit in the fridge overnight or serve immediately.

dressed brussels sprouts (half-cooked version)

¼ cup olive oil, divided

2 pounds Brussels sprouts, trimmed and thinly sliced

Salt

½ cup thick full-fat yogurt, such as Greek yogurt or skyr

1 tablespoon white miso paste

Juice of 1 lemon (about 3 tablespoons)

citrusy kale + brussels salad with parm + pistachios

Friends, it's time to pull out your big bowl for this one. Much like one of my favorite TV shows, *Derry Girls*, you need your big bowl. Borrow it from your neighbor like Mary or fish it out of its hiding place in the back of a closet—an ordinary bowl just won't do. Full of bright citrus flavors, this is just the salad you want for wintery days when citrus reigns supreme. Since it's raw, I love serving it with hot dishes that want this gentle and flavorful side dish that won't steal the show but will complement it perfectly instead. You can make it ahead for guests or to enjoy throughout the week, topping it with leftover chicken, shrimp, steak, or whatever you'd like. (Sliced avocado would also be a nice addition.)

Serve 6

2 teaspoons honey

2 teaspoons Dijon mustard

2 tablespoons grated Parmesan, plus more for garnish

½ teaspoon red pepper flakes

Juice of 1 large lemon (about 3 tablespoons)

Juice of 3 clementines or other small, sweet, tangerine-ish citrus (about ¼ cup)

3 tablespoons olive oil

1 bunch lacinato kale, leaves stemmed and thinly sliced

1 pound Brussels sprouts, trimmed and thinly sliced

1 bunch scallions, sliced

Salt

¼ cup shelled salted and roasted pistachios, roughly chopped

In your biggest salad bowl, use a fork to whisk together the honey, mustard, Parmesan, red pepper flakes, lemon juice, clementine juice, and olive oil until smooth. Add the kale, Brussels sprouts, and scallions and toss with clean hands to combine, scrunching everything together with the dressing to tenderize the kale and Brussels. Season to taste with salt. Cover and set aside for at least 30 minutes or refrigerate overnight. Top with the pistachios and a final sprinkle of Parmesan, and serve.

crunchy lettuce with sunflower seeds + sweet potatoes

I love the crunchy sunflower seeds in this recipe, so little that they disappear between the folds of the lettuce, some gathering at the bottom of the dish; they add so much flavor and texture when you find them. If you're serving this to guests, sprinkle half the seeds in when you toss the salad, then add the rest with the parsley as a garnish so they are still visually there.

Serves 2

1 small sweet potato, cut into ½-inch cubes (about 2 cups)

¼ cup olive oil, divided

¼ teaspoon ground cumin

Pinch of red pepper flakes

Salt

1 lime, halved

1 teaspoon sherry vinegar or red wine vinegar

2 teaspoons Dijon mustard

1 head Bibb or butter lettuce, leaves gently ripped in half or left whole

2 tablespoons sunflower seeds, lightly toasted (see note) and seasoned with salt

1 tablespoon packed fresh parsley, leaves and tender stems, gently chopped or torn

1 tablespoon grated Parmesan

Heat the oven to 400°F. On a sheet pan, toss the sweet potatoes with 2 tablespoons olive oil, cumin, and red pepper flakes and season lightly with salt. Roast until they are soft and creamy, about 25 minutes. Squeeze half a lime over the sweet potatoes and stir to coat. Let cool while you assemble the salad.

In a large serving bowl, combine the juice of the remaining lime half, the vinegar, mustard, and remaining olive oil until smooth. Season lightly with salt. Toss gently with the lettuce, sweet potatoes, and sunflower seeds. Top with the parsley and Parmesan, and serve.

note: You could use butternut squash in place of the sweet potato.

to lightly toast the seeds: put them in a dry pan over medium heat, stirring occasionally, until they start to color and are fragrant, 2 to 3 minutes.

skillet charred artichokes with red onion rings + lemony yogurt dip

Inspired by a delicious dish at Via Carota, this side dish (or appetizer) uses store-bought artichoke hearts, squeezes out any water or excess oil, then chars them in a pan along with the red onion rings. A hot, dry skillet is what helps to get the color on them, but keep in mind that your kitchen will get a little steamy. Artichoke jars come in all different sizes, so try to get as close as you can to the size called for here, but don't worry if it's off by a little. And if you don't manage perfect onion rings and they fall apart or are different thicknesses, all good, too.

½ cup thick full-fat yogurt, such as Greek yogurt or skyr

1 lemon, halved

¼ teaspoon red pepper flakes, plus more for the artichokes

2 tablespoons packed fresh parsley, finely chopped

Salt

2 (9.8-ounce) jars whole or halved artichoke hearts in water or oil

1 small red onion, cut into thin rings, core poked out

2 tablespoons olive oil

In a small serving bowl, mix the yogurt, the juice from one lemon half, the red pepper flakes, and half the parsley and season to taste with salt. Set in the fridge until ready to serve.

Use a clean dish towel or paper towel to press out any excess water or oil from the artichokes. Then quarter the whole ones and halve the halved ones, saving any pieces that fall off. Heat a dry 12-inch cast-iron or other heavy skillet over medium-high heat until very hot, about 2 minutes. Spread the onion rings out in a thin layer in the dry pan, season lightly with salt, and cook, without moving, for 2 minutes. Add the artichokes, season lightly with salt, and stir to combine with the onion. Cook, undisturbed, until charred in spots, about 4 minutes more, stirring halfway through. (Lower the heat if the onions threaten to burn.)

Lower the heat to medium and stir in the olive oil. Season lightly with salt and a pinch of red pepper flakes. Cook until the onions are silky, and a vibrant red color and the artichokes are browned in spots, 4 to 6 minutes more. Transfer to a plate, squeeze the remaining lemon half over everything, and garnish with the remaining parsley. Serve with the lemony yogurt.

roasted apricots with basil + feta

My colorful vision for the original version of this dish—crispy beef meatballs with thin, charred orange slices and juicy roasted apricots, all made on a sheet pan—was a bit of a fail as the meatballs didn't brown, and some of the meat juice muddled the colors. But, it was a happy failure as I realized it's a gorgeous side dish to pair with roast chicken or to eat for breakfast with toast and a spoonful of ricotta or other soft cheese and some black pepper. They, whoever they are, are right that you can learn from your mistakes! Use underripe apricots or any other large stone fruit, so they don't get mushy.

1 tablespoon olive oil

1 small navel orange, zested and ¼ juiced (about 1 tablespoon), then the remainder thinly sliced

1 tablespoon honey

6 or 7 small apricots, halved and pitted

½ cup crumbled feta cheese

¼ cup packed fresh basil leaves or mint, gently torn or chopped

Freshly cracked black pepper

Heat the oven to 400°F. Drizzle a sheet pan with the olive oil and use your hands to spread it out. In a small bowl, stir together the orange zest and juice, and the honey until mostly combined (the honey might not be perfectly combined and that's okay). Dip the apricots in the honey mixture to coat all over, then transfer to the prepared sheet pan, cut-side up, and add the orange slices.

Bake until the centers of the apricots are starting to look soft and jam-like and the edges are barely darkening in color, about 20 minutes. Sprinkle with the feta, basil, and a few grinds of pepper and serve.

lime-ginger roasted radishes

Red Cat, a now-defunct restaurant in New York's Chelsea neighborhood, used to serve radishes with salt at their bar as a snack, a very French thing to do, but it was the first time I had seen it. I instantly fell for the crunchy, salty bites, as it felt much lighter than chips or nuts, and a better preamble to the meal ahead. While you should definitely set some out for friends (maybe even with some nice salted butter), this roasted version gives you that same salty, snacky feel but leaves the radishes tasting more like potatoes, cutting through that innate pepperiness that they have. They still retain their beautiful color, so they make for a great snacking or side dish any time of year (especially to the sumac-dill salmon on page 148).

1 lime, halved, 1 half thinly sliced

1 teaspoon grated or minced fresh ginger (from a 1-inch piece)

3 scallions, thinly sliced

1 pound red radishes, trimmed and halved, larger ones quartered

Salt

2 tablespoons olive oil

Heat the oven to 400°F. On a sheet pan, combine the lime slices, ginger, most of the scallions, and radishes, season with salt, drizzle with the olive oil, and toss to coat.

Roast until the radishes are easily pierced with a fork, about 20 minutes, stirring halfway through. Squeeze the juice of the remaining lime half and remaining scallions on top and serve.

blistered sweet peppers with feta + mint

In full transparency, sweet peppers have never been my thing, but I once found myself at a friend's house who had a bag of them, and when she asked, "What should we do with these?" I must have given her a blank stare back, because she asked me again. The idea of blistering them in a pan, much like Padrón or shishito peppers, popped into my head. And here they are, highly snackable, colorful, and perfect as an appetizer or side dish. Some bread to soak up any melted feta and crispy bits on the bottom of the pan is always a good idea.

2 tablespoons olive oil

1 pound mini sweet peppers

Salt

¼ teaspoon red pepper flakes

1 lime, halved

½ cup crumbled feta, preferably Bulgarian

¼ cup packed fresh mint leaves, gently chopped or torn

Flaky sea salt

Heat the olive oil in a 12-inch skillet over medium-high heat until shimmering. Add the peppers, season with salt, and cook, undisturbed, for 2 minutes. Flip and cook for 2 minutes more, undisturbed, then flip and cook for another 2 to 3 minutes, until most are blistered on at least one side. They will start to pop and hop in the pan, which is fun, but watch out for any splattering oil. Add the red pepper flakes and the lime juice and toss to coat, about 30 seconds.

Remove from the heat and transfer to a plate, or serve from the hot pan. Sprinkle the feta on top, then let cool for a few minutes, which also lets the feta melt (wait to add the mint, or it will brown from the heat of the peppers). Finish with the mint and some flaky salt and enjoy.

vinegary brussels sprouts with pepperoni

I was house- and cat-sitting for my sister and her husband, and, like any normal human, I opened their fridge to see what awaited me once they'd left. Pepperoni! An entire container of these cute little cups. Hungry and feeling lazy, I decided to add them to a sheet pan of Broccolini. Some become crispy and crunchy, while others were soft and curled, their orange-tinted oil seeping out and coloring the sheet pan, kind of like pizza drippings. I've found that turkey pepperoni works just as well, if you prefer it.

1½ pounds Brussels sprouts, trimmed and halved, large ones quartered

Salt

2 tablespoons olive oil

2 ounces pepperoni (about ½ cup)

¼ cup grated Parmesan, plus more as needed

2 teaspoons sherry vinegar or red wine vinegar, or more as needed

Heat the oven to 400°F. On a sheet pan, season the Brussels sprouts with salt and drizzle with the olive oil. Roast until lightly browned, 20 to 25 minutes. Toss the pepperoni onto the sheet pan and roast until both the sprouts and the pepperoni are crispy and browned, 10 to 15 minutes more. Remove from the oven and toss with the Parmesan and vinegar on the sheet pan. Taste and add more vinegar, if needed. Finish with a final sprinkling of Parmesan, if desired.

see page 226 for recipe photo

garlicky greens

Make this easy, simple side of greens to round out any meal: serve with roast meats, pasta, salmon, or the lentil salad on page 212. It's warming, quick, and a nice green addition to the table on nights when it's too cold to serve salad. It might not steal the show, but it's a great, reliable companion.

1 tablespoon olive oil

kale or chard, kale leaves stemmed and roughly torn into large pieces, chard ends trimmed and stalks cut into small pieces (see page 111)

Salt

2 to 3 garlic cloves, thinly sliced (or smashed for less strong flavor)

Red pepper flakes

½ cup low-sodium vegetable broth or water (use leftover bits of broth from other recipes, if you have them)

1 tablespoon soy sauce, plus more as needed

1 lemon, halved

Freshly cracked black pepper

Heat the olive oil in a 12-inch skillet with a tight-fitting lid over medium-high heat until shimmering. Add the greens, season very lightly with salt (the soy sauce will add a lot of salt), and cook, stirring, until they have shrunken down slightly, about 3 minutes. Stir in the garlic and red pepper flakes (use anywhere from a pinch up to ¼ teaspoon, depending on your heat preference) and cook until fragrant, about 1 minute.

Pour in the broth and soy sauce, toss to combine, and cover. Adjust the heat to maintain an active simmer and cook until the greens are tender, about 6 minutes. Uncover and cook for about 2 minutes to let some liquid evaporate. Squeeze in half the lemon juice, then taste and season with more lemon juice and a splash more soy sauce, if needed. Finish with a few grinds of black pepper.

sticky-sweet roasted carrots with orange + pistachios

Such a Mediterranean dish! Guess where I first made it? Menorcan oranges are unbelievably flavorful, so I couldn't resist grabbing one last minute, slicing it, and adding it to the carrots. Thankfully, it worked out. The carrots are coated in an herb, spice, and honey mixture, which might sound odd, given that carrots are already sweet, but it works. You can also pop the carrots under the broiler, add the pistachios then, for a bit more toasty char on everything. Serving this on top of a honey-sweetened yogurt with orange juice (like on page 127) would also be delicious.

½ teaspoon red pepper flakes

½ teaspoon salt

1 tablespoon dried oregano

1 tablespoon honey

2 tablespoons olive oil, plus more for drizzling

1 bunch medium carrots, sliced lengthwise (thin ones can be kept whole)

1 small sweet orange, such as Cara Cara, sliced into rounds, any seeds poked out

4 or 5 garlic cloves, peeled and smashed

½ cup shelled salted pistachios, roughly chopped

¼ cup crumbled feta, preferably Bulgarian

Heat the oven to 400°F. In a small bowl, mix together the red pepper flakes, salt, oregano, honey, and olive oil until as smooth as possible (it won't be perfect). Add the carrots, orange slices, and garlic to a sheet pan and lightly drizzle with oil. Pour on the marinade and toss to coat, adding more oil as needed until everything has a light sheen to it. This part will be messy, but try approaching it with a playful, childlike attitude.

Roast until the carrots are easily pierced with a fork, about 30 minutes, then add the pistachios and cook for 5 minutes more. Sprinkle with the feta and serve.

crispy vinegary potatoes with miso + parmesan

A truly mouthwatering dish that's so easy to make, unless you mess it up like I did. One night, when making this, I greedily decided I wanted the potatoes even crispier when they were perfectly done, and, in what can only be described as carelessness, I didn't bother fully opening the oven door while holding the sheet pan with a kitchen towel, so I ended up bumping the sheet pan on a rack, which sent half of my glorious, stunning potatoes tumbling down onto the bottom of the oven. In addition to my shouts of despair, giant wafts of smoke began pouring out of the oven. So I shut it, opened all the windows and doors, and turned on my air purifier, shaking my head at myself for being a tired human, and then stress ate the surviving potatoes. It totally sucked. I wish you a better potato-cooking experience than mine, but know that these accidents happen to the best of us.

1½ to 2 pounds baby yellow potatoes, halved, large ones quartered

Salt

¼ teaspoon red pepper flakes

2 tablespoons olive oil, or more as needed

2 teaspoons white miso paste

1 tablespoon ghee or unsalted butter

1 teaspoon apple cider vinegar or sherry vinegar, plus more as needed

¼ cup grated Parmesan

Heat the oven to 400°F. On a sheet pan, season the potatoes with salt and red pepper flakes and coat with the olive oil. They should all look slick with oil, so add some more if needed until that happens. Roast until the potatoes are crispy on the outside and tender inside (pierce one to check), 40 to 55 minutes.

When the potatoes are nearly done, in a small bowl, mash together the miso and ghee (it won't be perfectly combined, and that's okay). Add the mixture to the hot sheet pan of cooked potatoes and toss to coat as it melts. Stir in the vinegar, taste, then season with more vinegar or salt, if needed; remembering that the cheese will add some salt, too. Sprinkle the Parmesan on top and serve.

cheesy potatoes in spiced tomato sauce

These saucy potatoes are perfect alongside roast chicken (you can cook in the oven together) or part of a vegetable spread. They are inspired by Spanish patatas bravas but are more swimming in a rich tomato sauce with bits of melty cheese than the traditional version. Serve leftovers crisped in a pan with eggs for breakfast or eat with some runny eggs for dinner.

1½ to 2 pounds baby yellow potatoes, halved, large ones quartered

¼ cup olive oil, divided, plus more as needed

Salt

1 (4.6-ounce) tube tomato paste (about ½ cup), preferably double-concentrated

1 teaspoon dried oregano

1 tablespoon piménton (smoked paprika)

1 tablespoon ground cumin

1 (28-ounce) can crushed tomatoes

1 tablespoon sherry vinegar or red wine vinegar

4 ounces Mahón cheese, queso fresco, or feta, cut into small cubes or crumbled

¼ cup packed fresh basil or parsley, leaves and tender stems, gently torn or chopped (optional)

Heat the oven to 400°F. On a sheet pan, combine the potatoes with 2 tablespoons of the olive oil, adding more as needed until all are slick with oil, then season with salt. Roast until browned and easily pierced with a fork, 40 to 55 minutes.

Once the potatoes are in the oven, heat the remaining oil over medium-high heat in a Dutch oven or 12-inch skillet until shimmering. Add the tomato paste, oregano, paprika, and cumin and cook, stirring continuously, until it becomes a fiery red color and smells fragrant, about 2 minutes. Pour in the crushed tomatoes and vinegar and season with salt. Bring the mixture to a boil, then lower the heat to maintain a gentle simmer with small bubbles forming across the surface. Cover and cook, stirring occasionally, until the potatoes are ready.

Stir in the roasted potatoes and cook over low heat, uncovered, for 5 minutes. Remove from the heat, then stir in the cheese, letting it melt and the potatoes cool for 5 minutes. Top with the basil, if desired, and serve.

all the thank-yous!

Trust is one of the greatest gifts to receive, so thank you to everyone at Harper for trusting me fully with this book: Julie Will for believing in me and this idea, Karen Rinaldi for your unwavering support no matter what happened, Kirby Sandmeyer and Emma Kupor for your help as well. Yelena Nesbit and Leslie Cohen, I feel lucky to be in your smart and capable hands. Thank you to Amanda Pritzker and Jessica Gilo for getting this book out into the world, and to everyone else at Harper who have helped on the journey from this book being a bunch of documents on my computer to the beautiful one you're holding in your hands today.

Kari Stuart, I truly hope you don't dread seeing my name in your inbox because there have been so many emails from me! I cannot express how much I appreciate your steadiness, good humor, and support. A huge thank-you and hug along with it! Thank you as well to Tia Ikemoto and Phoebe Rhinehart for fielding my other numerous emails and always patiently and kindly responding, and to everyone else at CAA for your support.

The moments when you ask for help are when you truly realize how deeply loved and supported you are, and I could not be more thankful or grateful for the people that I'm lucky enough to call friends. When I asked for recipe-testing help, I was blown away by the response and deeply and heart-meltingly moved as I went through your thoughtful and detailed notes to each recipe. They are home-cook-friendly and accessible because of your questions and comments. And getting kid approval always makes me feel like it's a home run. So thank you, in no particular order, to Diana Perez + family, Joanna + the Novick + Schwartz family (including little Annabelle), Nicole Jackson (and Finn!), Sachié Alessio, Amanda Bassen (and Ava for her egg-free meatball inspiration), Ana Drabek + Joni Colburn, Rebecca Clareman, Matthew Cherner-Ranft, Laura + Andy Sweeting, Ben Israel, Jess Goldman Foung, Molly Ahuja (and little Havi!), Lesley Tellez, Shannon Paz, Julia Clancy, Hannah Howard + Rachel Howard, Jennifer Bruno, Lizzie Gahagan + family, Ashley Fahr, and everyone else who tried and tasted these dishes! You make my heart full. :)

Lisa Nicklin, I love working with you as you truly make each recipe you touch better than it was—I know I've said this before, but it's true! And I appreciate your kindly telling me when something isn't working, despite my stubbornness to make it work.

For the props in this book (linens, cutlery, pots, and so on), I tried to use the brands that I love and use in my own kitchen, so a huge thank-you to everyone who donated or lent items for us to use: Le Creuset, your generosity and kindness was truly touching and appreciated. Atelier Saucier, thank you for always answering my last-minute, panicky emails for requests—your linens are as fun and lovely as you two are and always make my kitchen a happier place. Robert Siegel, I'm glad we're related because I will forever be using your beautiful ceramics (and asking for a family discount, thank you!). Madre Linen, thank you for sending over some linens for us to use. Fish

Wife, your tinned goods are so good. The Boardsmith, thank you for the gorgeous cutting board gracing some of the photos in the book!

Matt Russell, I feel very lucky to have your beautiful photos fill this book and to have gotten to know you; as you are equally as lovely as your work. Your photography is stunning, and the care, thought, and detail you put into your work are both impressive and inspiring. You are simply the best! And thank you for tolerating me, Nicole, and our sense of humor. Lads! Nicole Herft, thank you as always for your enthusiasm and skilled hand in plating my food so well. Paru Frances, where would we have been without you? Truly lost. Thank you for joining our small team.

Allegra Angelo, I'm so happy we met those 12 to 15 (?) years ago, and thank you for creating such a thoughtful and helpful wine guide for readers. You truly know your stuff!

The stunning cover, wine chart and illustrations throughout the book are thanks to the talented Evi-O Studio team, including Evi O., Susan Lee, and Pamela Surly. Bonni Leon-Berman, thank you for your patience and kindness in working with me and in creating the interior of this book. Feeling very lucky to have worked on this together. And to Milan Bozic, thank you for leading the charge and helping us get to where we needed to go with this beautiful cover.

To the friends who support me in other ways and warm my heart for being in my life, thank you!! Ali Rosen, Annie Daly, Cheryl Chan + Tom Cornett, Michael + Juan Manatos-McCafferty, Sally Averill, Ben Bernstein + Nichole Ferrera, Ian Pilarski, Leyla + Darvish Fakhr. And to my wonderful neighbors in Miami, Karla + Scott McMullen and Mirella Quadri, for trying so many of my dishes, taking care of my plant babies when I went away, and making my time there so special.

To all of the wonderful editors and colleagues whom I've worked with over the years, thank you so much for your guidance, teachings, and support. Especially everyone at *New York Times* Cooking: you shaped my career in an invaluable way, and I will forever be grateful.

My lovely Pingo, you were an angel on this earth who is deeply missed, thank you for loving me so much. Mark Edgar Stephens, I am so lucky that we met and so deeply grateful for your calm, kind, and loving presence in my life.

Ashley Fahr, my darling sister, thank you for generously letting us use La Cuisine for the photo shoot and tolerating our moving pretty much everything around in the Mug Shop, before we put it back to how it was—more or less. And for gracing us with your beautiful arm and hand for the third chapter opener. Love you so much!

To my wonderful parents, you are true daughter-supporters through and through! Thank you for instilling a love for food and life in me. And, you know, all the other things, too :).

Thank you to everyone reading this far and buying this book and supporting me—you make it all worthwhile! Ending as we started, thank you for trusting me with your time and well-being and letting me join you around the dinner table—however that looks!

I am so lucky for each and every one of you.

Thank you all! xx

bibliography + inspiration

Thank you to the wonderful writers of these books for providing me with inspiration, factual knowledge, and sometimes reassurance that I'm not losing my mind. I highly recommend learning and cooking from all these beautiful books. To a certain extent, there's nothing *new* in cooking–there have been many tomato sauces before mine– and while I do my best to make the recipes feel like me, putting my own spin on them, I would be remiss not to thank all those who came before me and the talented recipe developers who work alongside me and inspire me daily.

Science in the Kitchen and the Art of Eating Well, Pellegrino Artusi
Salted, Mark Bitterman
How to Cook Everything Vegetarian, Mark Bittman
Chez Panisse Vegetables, Alice Waters
Paula Wolfert + books
Claudia Roden + books
Tender, Nigel Slater
On Food and Cooking, Harold McGee
Food Lover's Companion, Sharon Tyler Herbst
How to Eat, Nigella Lawson

Also thank you to all the home cooks (especially *New York Times* commenters–I love reading your notes!) for your messages and feedback. I take them very seriously and find them extremely helpful!

Index

(Page numbers in *italics* refer to photographs and numbers in **bold** refer to swaps.)

about the author

YASMIN FAHR is a food writer and recipe developer who has a penchant for cheesy phrases, lemons, fresh herbs, feta, and cumin (as you'll soon see). A frequent contributor to *New York Times* Cooking and the author of *Keeping It Simple* and *Boards & Spreads*, she attended Cornell University and then completed a master's degree in food studies from New York University. She is currently on a quest to move to Menorca, with previous stints, both lengthy and brief, in New York City, Los Angeles, London, and Miami. Please say hi to her online at @yasminfahr and www.yasminfahr.co/.

HarperCollins books may be purchased for educational, business, or sales promotional use. For information, please email the Special Markets Department at SPsales@harpercollins.com.

FIRST EDITION

Designed by Bonni Leon-Berman

Photography by Matt Russell

Illustrations by Evi-O Studio

Library of Congress Cataloging-in-Publication Data has been applied for.

ISBN 978-0-06-328417-3

24 25 26 27 28   TC   10 9 8 7 6 5 4 3 2 1